A New Generation Draws the Line

Humanitarian Intervention and the "Responsibility to Protect" Today

NOAM CHOMSKY

Expanded Edition

Paradigm Publishers
Boulder • London

Copyright © 2001, 2012 by Noam Chomsky.

Published in the United States by Paradigm Publishers, 2845 Wilderness Place, Boulder, CO 80301 USA.

Some portions of this book were published in an earlier version, *A New Generation Draws the Line: Kosovo, East Timor and the Standards of the West*, by Noam Chomsky (Verso 2001.)

Paradigm Publishers is the trade name of Birkenkamp & Company, LLC, Dean Birkenkamp, President and Publisher.

Hardcover ISBN: 978-1-61205-073-7 Paperback ISBN: 978-1-61205-074-4

The Library of Congress Cataloging-in-Publication Data for this title is available from the Library of Congress.

Printed and bound in the United States of America on acid-free paper that meets the standards of the American National Standard for Permanence of Paper for Printed Library Materials.

Designed and typeset by Straight Creek Bookmakers.

16 15 14 13 12   1 2 3 4 5

Contents

Foreword

This book deals with the new interventionism of the Western powers, mostly of the United States.

These interventions are repeatedly justified on grounds of the "right (or duty) of humanitarian intervention" or the "responsibility to protect" – publicized as R2P[1]. This ideology justifying intervention was developed following the end of the Vietnam War and the collapse of the European colonial empires. It drew on the tragedies that occurred in the newly independent countries, starting with the "boat people" in Vietnam and the "killing fields" of the Khmer Rouge in Cambodia, and later with the events in Rwanda and Yugoslavia, to justify intervention, including military intervention, by Western powers in the internal affairs of the rest of the world. NATO bombing of Yugoslavia and more recently of Libya was justified on that basis. The wars in Afghanistan and in Iraq were justified on more traditional pretexts of "national security" (including, in the case of Iraq, a preventive strike against hypothetical weapons of mass destruction), but arguments based on the idea of humanitarian intervention, such as protecting Afghan women or toppling a dictator, were also used to gain support from left-liberal opinion in Western countries.

The humanitarian rhetoric was particularly strident at the beginning of the 2011 Libyan war, not least within the European left, where we were told that we must "do something" even if it means "allying with the devil" (the United States, NATO, Sarkozy, and company) in order to stop the "dictator" from "murdering his own people". Anyone opposed to, or even just lukewarm about, this intervention risked being considered an accomplice of the dictator, and retrospectively guilty of Munich, of refusing to support the Spanish Republic, or of abandoning the Jews to their fate during World War II.

The main target of the humanitarian interventionists is the concept of national sovereignty, on which the current international law is based, and which they stigmatize as allowing dictators to kill their own people at will. The impression is sometimes given that national sovereignty is nothing but a protection for dictators whose only desire is to kill their own people.

But in fact, the primary justification of national sovereignty is precisely to provide at least a partial protection of weak states against strong ones. A state that is strong enough can do whatever it chooses without worrying about intervention from outside. Nobody expects Bangladesh to interfere in the internal affairs of the United States in order to force it to reduce its CO_2 emissions, which threaten to drown large parts of that Asian country. Nobody is going to bomb the United States to force it to modify its immigration or monetary policies because of the human consequences of such policies on other countries. Humanitarian intervention goes only one way: from the powerful to the weak.

The very starting point of the United Nations was to save humankind from "the scourge of war," with reference to the two world wars. This was to be done precisely by strict respect for national sovereignty, in order to prevent Great Powers from intervening militarily against weaker ones, regardless of the pretext. The protection of national sovereignty in international law was based on recognition that internal conflicts in weak countries can be exploited by strong ones, as was shown by Germany's interventions in Czechoslovakia and Poland ostensibly "in defense of oppressed minorities," which led to World War II.

Then came decolonization. Following World War II, dozens of newly independent countries freed themselves from the colonial yoke. The last thing they wanted was to see former colonial powers openly interfering in their internal affairs (even though such interference has often persisted in more-or-less veiled forms, notably in African countries). This aversion to foreign interference explains why the "right" of humanitarian intervention has been universally rejected by the countries of the South, for example at the South Summit in Havana in April 2000. Meeting in Kuala Lumpur in February 2003, shortly before the US attack on Iraq, "The Heads of State or Government reiterated the rejection by the Non-Aligned Movement of the so-called 'right' of humanitarian intervention, which has no basis either in United Nations Charter or in international law"; and "also observed similarities between the new expression 'responsibility to protect' and 'humanitarian intervention' and requested the Co-ordinating Bureau to carefully study and consider the expression 'the responsibility to protect' and its implications on the basis of the principles of non-interference and non-intervention as well as the respect for territorial integrity and national sovereignty of States."

The main failure of the United Nations has not been that it did not stop dictators from murdering their own people, but that it failed to prevent powerful countries from violating the principles of international law: the United States in Indochina and Iraq, South Africa in Angola and Mozambique, Israel in its neighboring countries, Indonesia in East Timor; not to speak of all the coups, threats, embargoes, unilateral sanctions, bought elections, and so on. Many millions of people lost their lives because of such repeated violation of international law and of the principle of national sovereignty.

In a post–World War II history that includes the Indochina wars; the invasions of Iraq and Afghanistan, of Panama, and even of tiny Grenada; as well as the bombing of Yugoslavia, Libya, and various other countries, it is scarcely credible to maintain that it is international law and respect for national sovereignty that prevent the United States from stopping genocide. If the United States had had the means and the desire to intervene in Rwanda, it would have done so, and no international law would have prevented that. And if a "new norm" is introduced, such as the right of humanitarian intervention or the responsibility to protect, within the context of the current relationship of political and military forces, it will not save anyone anywhere, unless the United States sees fit to intervene, from its own perspective.

US interference in the internal affairs of other states is multi-faceted but constant, and repeatedly violates the spirit and often the letter of the UN Charter. Despite claims to act on behalf of principles such as freedom and democracy, US intervention has repeatedly had disastrous consequences: not only the millions of deaths caused by direct and indirect wars, but also the lost opportunities for hundreds of millions of people who might have benefited from progressive social policies initiated by leaders such as Arbenz in Guatemala, Goulart in Brazil, Allende in Chile, Lumumba in the Congo, Mossadegh in Iran, the Sandinistas in Nicaragua, or President Chavez in Venezuela, who have been systematically subverted, overthrown, or killed with full Western support.

But that is not all. Every aggressive action led by the United States creates a reaction. Deployment of an anti-missile shield produces more missiles, not fewer. Bombing civilians – whether deliberately or by so-called "collateral damage" – produces more armed resistance, not less.

Trying to overthrow or subvert governments produces more internal repression, not less. Encouraging secessionist minorities by giving them the often false impression that the sole Superpower will come to their rescue in case they are repressed leads to more violence, hatred, and death, not less. Surrounding a country with military bases produces more defense spending by that country, not less, and the possession of nuclear weapons by Israel encourages other states of the Middle East to acquire such weapons.

Moreover, the humanitarian disasters in Eastern Congo are mainly due to foreign interventions (mostly from Rwanda, a

US ally), not to a lack of them. To take a most extreme case, which is a favorite example of horrors cited by advocates of the humanitarian interventions, it is most unlikely that the Khmer Rouge would ever have taken power in Cambodia without the massive "secret" US bombing followed by US-engineered regime change that left that unfortunate country totally disrupted and destabilized.

Another problem with the "right of humanitarian intervention" is that it fails to suggest any principle to replace national sovereignty. When NATO exercised its own self-proclaimed right to intervene in Kosovo, where diplomatic efforts were far from having been exhausted, it was praised by the Western media. When Russia exercised what it regarded as its own R2P in South Ossetia, it was uniformly condemned in the same Western media.

When Vietnam intervened in Cambodia to put an end to the Khmer Rouge, or India intervened to free Bangladesh from Pakistan, their actions were also harshly condemned in the United States. So either every country with the means to do so acquires the right to intervene whenever a humanitarian reason can be invoked as a justification, and we are back to the war of all against all, or only an all-powerful state, namely the United States (and its allies) are allowed to do so, and we are back to a form of dictatorship in international affairs.

It is often said that the interventions are not to be carried out by one state, but by the "international community." The concept of "international community" is used primarily by the United States and its allies to designate themselves and whoever agrees with them at the time. It has grown into a concept that both rivals the United Nations (the "international community" claims to be more "democratic" than many UN member states) and tends to take it over in many ways.

In reality, there is no such thing as a genuine international community. NATO's intervention in Kosovo was not approved by Russia, and Russian intervention in South Ossetia was condemned by the West. There would have been no Security Council approval for either intervention. The African Union has rejected the indictment by the International Criminal Court of the President of Sudan. Most of the world – Latin America, India, Russia, China – does not approve of NATO's war against Libya, despite the UNSC Resolution 1973. Any system of international justice or police, whether it is R2P or the ICC, would need to be based on a relationship of equality and a climate of trust. Today, there is no equality and no trust, between West and East, between North and South, largely as a result of the record of US policies. For some version of R2P to be consensually functional in the future, we need first to build a relationship of equality and trust.

The Libyan adventure has illustrated another reality conveniently overlooked by the supporters of humanitarian intervention, namely that without the huge US military machine, the sort of safe no-casualty (on our side) intervention that can hope to gain public support is not possible.

The Western countries are not willing to risk sacrificing too many lives of their troops, and waging a purely aerial war requires an enormous amount of high technology equipment. Those who support such interventions are supporting, whether they realize it or not, the continued existence of the US military machine, with its bloated budgets and its weight on the national debt. The European Greens and Social Democrats who support the war in Libya should have the honesty to tell their constituents that they need to accept massive cuts in public spending on pensions, unemployment, health care, and education in order to bring such social expenses down to an American level and use the hundreds of billions of euros thus saved to build a military machine that will be able to intervene whenever and wherever there is humanitarian crisis.

If it is true that the 21st century needs a new United Nations, it does not need one that legitimizes such interventions by novel arguments, such as R2P, but one that gives at least moral support to those who try to construct a world less dominated by a single military superpower. The United Nations needs to pursue its efforts to achieve its founding purpose before setting a new, supposedly humanitarian priority, which may in reality be used by the Great Powers to justify their own future wars by undermining the principle of national sovereignty.

There should be an active peace policy through international cooperation, disarmament, and non-intervention of states in the internal affairs of others. We could use our overblown military budgets to implement a form of global Keynesianism: Instead of demanding "balanced budgets" in the developing world, we should use the resources wasted on our military to finance massive investments in education, health care, and development. If this sounds utopian, it is not more so than the belief that a stable world will emerge from the way our current "war on terror" is being carried out.

Moreover, one should strive toward strict respect for international law on the part of Western powers; implementing the

UN resolutions concerning Israel; dismantling the worldwide US empire of bases as well as NATO; ceasing all threats concerning the unilateral use of force; stopping all interference in the internal affairs of other States, in particular all operations of "democracy promotion," "color" revolutions, and the exploitation of the politics of minorities. This necessary respect for national sovereignty means that the ultimate sovereign of each nation-state is the people of that state, whose right to replace unjust governments cannot be taken over by supposedly benevolent outsiders.

It will be objected that such a policy would allow dictators to "murder their own people," the current slogan justifying intervention. But if non-intervention may allow such terrible things to happen, history shows that military intervention frequently has the same result, when cornered leaders and their followers turn their wrath on the "traitors" supporting foreign intervention. On the other hand, non-intervention spares domestic oppositions from being regarded as fifth columns of the Western powers – an inevitable result of our interventionist policies. Actively seeking peaceful solutions would allow a reduction of military expenditures, arms sales (including to dictators who may use them to "murder their own people"), and use of resources to improve social standards.

Coming to the present situation, one must acknowledge that the West has been supporting Arab dictators for a variety of reasons, ranging from oil to Israel, in order to control that region; and that this policy is slowly collapsing. But the lesson to draw is not to rush into yet another war, in Libya, claiming this time to be on the right side, defending the people against dictators, but to recognize that it is high time for us to stop assuming that we must control the Arab world. At the dawn of the 20th century, most of the world was under European control. Eventually, the West will lose control over that part of the world, as it lost it in East Asia and is losing it in Latin America. How the West will adapt itself to its decline is the crucial political question of our time; answering it is unlikely to be either easy or pleasant.

The ideology of humanitarian intervention is part of a long history of Western attitudes toward the rest of the world. When Western colonialists landed on the shores of the Americas, Africa, or Eastern Asia, they were shocked by what we would now call violations of human rights, and which they called "barbaric mores": human sacrifices, cannibalism, women forced to bind their feet. Time and again, such indignation, sincere or calculating, has been used to justify or to cover up the crimes of the Western powers: the slave trade, the extermination of indigenous peoples, and the systematic stealing of land and resources. This attitude of righteous indignation continues to this day and is at the root of the claim that the West has a "right to intervene" and a "right to protect" while turning a blind eye to oppressive regimes considered "our friends," to endless militarization and wars, and to massive exploitation of labor and resources.

The promoters of humanitarian intervention present it as the beginning of a new era, but in fact it is the end of an old one. From an interventionist viewpoint, this doctrine backtracks with respect to the "rights" invoked by traditional colonialists. Millions of people, including American citizens, reject war as a means to settle international disputes and strongly oppose the blind support of their country for Israeli Apartheid. They adhere to the goals of the non-aligned movement of international cooperation within the strict respect for national sovereignty and equality of all peoples. They risk being denounced in the media of their own countries as being anti-Western. Yet they are the ones who, by opening their minds to the aspirations of the rest of mankind, carry on what is genuinely of value in the Western humanist tradition.

The major social transformation of the 20th century has been decolonization. It continues today in the elaboration of a genuinely democratic world, one in which the sun will have set on the US empire, just as it did on the old European ones.

Jean Bricmont
July 2011

Note

1. At the *2005 World Summit*, Member States included RtoP in the Outcome Document (*http://www.who.int/hiv/universalaccess2010/worldsummit.pdf*) in paragraphs 138 and 139 that state:

138. Each individual State has the responsibility to protect its populations from genocide, war crimes, ethnic cleansing and crimes against humanity. This responsibility entails the prevention of such crimes, including their incitement, through appropriate and necessary means. We accept that responsibility and will act in accordance with it. The international community should, as appropriate, encourage and help States to exercise this responsibility

and support the United Nations in establishing an early warning capability.

139. The international community, through the United Nations, also has the responsibility to use appropriate diplomatic, humanitarian and other peaceful means, in accordance with Chapters VI and VIII of the Charter, to help protect populations from genocide, war crimes, ethnic cleansing and crimes against humanity. In this context, we are prepared to take collective action, in a timely and decisive manner, through the Security Council, in accordance with the Charter, including Chapter VII, on a case-by-case basis and in cooperation with relevant regional organizations as appropriate, should peaceful means be inadequate and national authorities manifestly fail to protect their populations from genocide, war crimes, ethnic cleansing and crimes against humanity. We stress the need for the General Assembly to continue consideration of the responsibility to protect populations from genocide, war crimes, ethnic cleansing and crimes against humanity and its implications, bearing in mind the principles of the Charter and international law. We also intend to commit ourselves, as necessary and appropriate, to helping States build capacity to protect their populations from genocide, war crimes, ethnic cleansing and crimes against humanity and to assisting those which are under stress before crises and conflicts break out.

CHAPTER ONE

Intentional Ignorance and Its Uses

The twentieth century ended with terrible crimes, and reactions by the great powers that were widely heralded as opening a remarkable "new era" in human affairs, marked by dedication to human rights and high principle with no historical precedent. The torrent of self-adulation, which may well have been unprecedented in scale and quality, was not merely a display of millenarian rhetorical flourishes. Western leaders and intellectuals assured their audiences emphatically that the new era was very real, and of unusual significance.

The new phase in human history opened with NATO's bombing of Serbia on March 24 1999. "The new generation draws the line," Tony Blair proclaimed, fighting "for values," for "a new internationalism where the brutal repression of whole ethnic groups will no longer be tolerated" and "those responsible for such crimes have nowhere to hide." NATO has unleashed the first war in history fought "in the name of principles and values," Vaclav Havel declared, signalling "the end of the nation-state," which will no longer be "the culmination of every national community's history and its highest earthly value." The "enlightened efforts of generations of democrats, the terrible experience of two world wars, . . . and the evolution of civilization have finally brought humanity to the recognition that human beings are more important than the state."[1]

The new generation is to carry out its good works under the guiding hand of an "idealistic New World bent on ending inhumanity," joined by its British partner. In the lead article in *Foreign Affairs*, a legal scholar with a distinguished record in defending human rights explained that the "enlightened states," freed at last from the shackles of "restrictive old rules" and archaic concepts of world order, may now use force when they "believe it to be just," obeying "modern notions of justice" that they fashion as they discipline "the defiant, the indolent, and the miscreant," the "disorderly" elements of the world, with a nobility of purpose so "evident" that it requires no evidence.[2] The grounds for membership in the club of enlightened states – "the international community," as they conventionally describe themselves – are also self-evident. Past and current practice are boring old tales that may be dismissed under the doctrine of "change of course," which has been regularly invoked when needed in recent years.

Praising NATO troops in Macedonia for their achievement in opening the new era, President Clinton "propounded a Clinton Doctrine of military intervention," Bob Davis reported in the *Wall Street Journal*. The Doctrine "amounts to the following: Tyrants Beware." In the President's own words: "If somebody comes after innocent civilians and tries to kill them en masse because of their race, their ethnic background or their religion, and it's within our power to stop it, we will stop it"; "where we can make a difference, we must try, and that is clearly the case in Kosovo." "There are times when looking away simply is not an option," the President explained to the nation; "we can't respond to every tragedy in every corner of the world," but that doesn't mean that "we should do nothing for no one."[3]

Well before the dawn of the new era, Clinton's "neo-Wilsonianism" had convinced observers that American foreign policy had entered a "noble phase" with a "saintly glow," though some saw dangers from the outset, warning that by "granting idealism a near exclusive hold on our foreign policy" we might neglect our own interests in the service of others. Clinton's "open-ended embrace of humanitarian intervention" in 1999 also "has worried foreign-policy experts inside the administration and out," Davis reported. Senator John McCain derided it as "foreign policy as social work"; others agreed. To alleviate such concerns, Clinton's National Security Adviser Sandy Berger underscored the fact that ethnic cleansing, which "happens in dozens of countries around the world," cannot be the occasion for intervention. In Kosovo, US national interest was at stake: intervention "involved bolstering the credibility of NATO and making sure Kosovar refugees didn't overwhelm neighboring countries" – as they did shortly after the NATO bombing commenced, eliciting the massive ethnic cleansing that was an anticipated consequence. We are left, then, with "bolstering the credibility of NATO" as the surviving justification.[4]

Washington's official version, which has remained fairly constant throughout, was reiterated in January 2000 by Secretary of Defense William Cohen and Chairman of the Joint Chiefs of

Staff Henry Shelton, in a lengthy summary of the war provided to Congress. The US and NATO had three primary interests: "Ensuring the stability of Eastern Europe," "Thwarting ethnic cleansing," and "Ensuring NATO's credibility." Prime Minister Blair adopted the same stance[5]:

> The bottom line was we couldn't lose. If we lost, it's not just that we would have failed in our strategic objective; failed in terms of the moral purpose – we would have dealt a devastating blow to the credibility of NATO and the world would have been less safe as a result of that.

Let us put aside until later a closer look at the official positions, and ask how the world outside the "international community" understands NATO's efforts to assure its safety. Some insight into the matter was provided in April 2000 at the South Summit of G-77, accounting for 80 per cent of the world's population. The meeting, in Havana, was of unusual significance, the first meeting ever of G-77 (now 133 nations) at the level of heads of state, prepared shortly before by a summit of foreign ministers in Cartagena, Colombia. They issued the Declaration of the South Summit, declaring that "We reject the so-called 'right' of humanitarian intervention," along with other forms of coercion that the Summit also sees as traditional imperialism in a new guise, including the specific forms of corporate-led international integration called "globalization" in Western ideology.[6]

The most respected voices of the South joined in condemnation of NATO's operative principles. Visiting England in

April 2000, Nelson Mandela "accused the [British] government of encouraging international chaos, together with America, by ignoring other nations and playing 'policeman of the world'," saying that "he resented the behaviour of both Britain and America in riding roughshod over the United Nations and launching military actions against Iraq and Kosovo." "Such disregard for international conventions was more dangerous to world peace than anything that was currently happening in Africa, Mr Mandela said." In his own words, "What they are doing is far more serious than what is happening in Africa – especially the US and Britain. It is proper for me to say that."[7]

While in progress a year earlier, NATO's bombing of Yugoslavia had been bitterly condemned in the world's largest democracy, and even in Washington's most loyal and dependent client state, highly regarded strategic analysts regarded the operation with considerable skepticism. Amos Gilboa described NATO's reversion to the "colonial era" in the familiar "cloak of moralistic righteousness" as "a danger to the world," warning that it would lead to proliferation of weapons of mass destruction for deterrence. Others simply took it to be a precedent for resort to force when deemed appropriate. If the need arises, military historian Ze'ev Schiff commented, "Israel will do to Lebanon what NATO did to Kosovo"; Israeli forces are being restructured for quick and destructive air war, relying particularly on the Kosovo precedent. Similar attitudes were expressed in the semi-official press of the second leading recipient of US aid, and elsewhere.[8]

Among East European dissidents, the one most prominently featured in the West was Vaclav Havel, with his welcome appreciation for the high moral purpose of Western leaders. Long before, he had achieved top rank among the West's favorites, particularly in 1990, when he addressed a joint session of Congress, receiving a standing ovation and rapturous acclaim from commentators who were deeply moved by his praise for his audience as "the defender of freedom" who "understood the responsibility that flowed" from power. A few weeks before, the responsibility had been demonstrated once again when US-armed state terrorists fresh from renewed US training blew out the brains of six leading Latin American dissident intellectuals in the course of yet another paroxysm of terror supervised by "the defender of freedom." One can imagine the reaction to a similar performance in the Duma by a Latin American dissident, had the situation been reversed. The reaction in the West in this case is instructive, and not without import.[9]

There once was a dissident intellectual named Alexander Solzhenitsyn, who was also highly respected when he had the right things to say. But not in 1999. He saw the new era rather in the manner of the South Summit, Mandela, and others outside of the circles of enlightenment:

> The aggressors have kicked aside the UN, opening a new era where might is right. There should be no illusions that NATO was aiming to defend the Kosovars. If the protection of the oppressed was their real concern, they could have been defending for example the miserable Kurds

– "for example," because that is only one case, though a rather striking one.[10]

Solzhenitsyn remains a man "whom many see as the country's voice of conscience," admired for his "elegant and reasoned style" when he condemns government corruption in Russia.[11] But not when he provides the wrong interpretation of the new era. In this case, he received the same treatment as the South Summit, and others who do not see the light.

Though unwanted world opinion has scarcely been reported, it has been watched with concern by more perceptive analysts. University of Chicago political scientist John Mearsheimer observed that the Gulf war of 1991 and the Kosovo war of 1999 "hardened India's determination to possess nuclear weapons" as a deterrent to US violence. Harvard government professor Samuel Huntington warned that "in the eyes of many countries" – most, he indicates – the US "is becoming the rogue superpower," perceived as "the single greatest external threat to their societies." He quotes a British diplomat who says, "One reads about the world's desire for American leadership only in the United States," while "[e]verywhere else one reads about American arrogance and unilateralism," which will lead to consolidation of counterforces, Huntington suggests. Five years earlier, shortly after publicity about a possible North Korean nuclear arsenal, "the Japanese named the United States as 'the biggest threat to world peace,' followed by Russia and only then by North Korea," Chalmers Johnson recalls. During the Kosovo war, strategic analyst and former NATO planner Michael MccGwire writes,

the world at large saw a political-military alliance that took unto itself the role of judge, jury and executioner, . . .

[which] claimed to be acting on behalf of the international community and was ready to slight the UN and skirt international law in order to enforce its collective judgement. The world saw an organization given to moralistic rhetoric, one no less economical with the truth than others of its kind; a grouping of Western states with an unmatched technical capacity to kill, maim, and destroy, that was limited only by their unwillingness to put their "warriors" at risk.

That seems a fair assessment, judging by the information available.[12]

The world at large does not seem to be overly impressed by the exploits and moral purpose of the new generation, or reassured by its commitment to make the world safe by establishing the credibility of NATO. If evidence is deemed relevant, we may ask which evaluation of the new era is more credible: the flattering self-image with its visionary promise, or the skepticism of those outside who see "more of the same."

The matter should be examined carefully, at least by those who are concerned about the likely future, and who feel bound by moral truisms. Among these, several might be mentioned as particularly pertinent:

1. People are responsible for the anticipated consequences of their choice of action (or inaction), a responsibility that extends to the policy choices of one's own state to the extent that the political community allows a degree of influence over policy formation.

2. Responsibility is enhanced by privilege, by the opportunity to act with relative impunity and a degree of effectiveness.

3. For profession of high principles to be taken seriously, the principles must first and foremost be applied to oneself, not only to official enemies or others designated as unworthy in the prevailing political culture.

Let us assume the truisms to be true. It is, however, hard to miss the fact that throughout history, and in virtually all societies, they are commonly honored in the breach. A fair question, then, is whether the familiar pattern was exhibited once again in the terminal year of the twentieth century, as most of the world seems to believe, or whether a new era has really dawned, as the new generation and its admirers declare.

One question that instantly comes to mind is how often, and how carefully, the inquiry is undertaken. Rarely, to my knowledge: the conclusions are taken to be self-evident. No inquiry is needed, and even to undertake it is considered dishonorable.

It is clear how such an inquiry should proceed. To determine who has the stronger case, those who hail the new era or the skeptics, we should examine how the new generation responds to circumstances in the world "where we can make a difference" and therefore "must try," as Clinton phrased the matter in propounding the Clinton Doctrine.

We therefore consider various measures of US involvement in the world. One criterion is foreign aid: the world's richest and most privileged state would surely be able to "make a difference" by helping those in need. The political leadership has taken up this challenge by compiling the most miserly record in the industrial world, even if we include the major component, aid to a rich country (Israel) and to Egypt because of its association with Israel. As the new era dawns, the record is becoming still worse. The Foreign Aid Bill passed by the Senate in June 2000 "provided only $75 million for the world's poorest countries, a reduction from the administration's $252 million request," a shameful pittance.[13] In comparison, the Bill provides $1.3 billion for the Colombian army, a matter to which we return. Without proceeding, by this criterion the evaluation of the skeptics is confirmed, with no contest.

Perhaps this criterion is irrelevant for some (unclear) reason. Let us put it aside, then, and turn to the next natural criteria: military aid and response to atrocities. The top-ranking recipient of US military aid through the Clinton years has been Turkey,[14] the home of 15 million of Solzhenitsyn's "miserable Kurds." That seems an appropriate place to begin.

At the peak of enthusiasm over our dedication to principles and values, in April 1999, NATO commemorated its fiftieth anniversary. It was not a celebration; rather, a somber occasion, under the shadow of vicious atrocities and ethnic cleansing in Kosovo. It was agreed that the "modern notions of justice" crafted by the enlightened states do not permit such horrors so close to the borders of NATO. Only *within* the borders of NATO: here large-scale atrocities and ethnic cleansing are not only tolerable, but it is furthermore our duty to expedite them. We must not merely "stand by and watch the systematic state-directed murder of other people," but must go on to make an essential contribution to ensuring that it reaches proper heights of terror and destruction, while directing our gaze with laser-like intensity to the evil work of official enemies.

It took considerable discipline at the NATO anniversary for participants and commentators "not to notice" that some of the worst ethnic cleansing of the 1990s was taking place within NATO itself, in south-eastern Turkey; and furthermore, that these massive atrocities relied on a huge flow of arms from the West, overwhelmingly from the United States, which provided about 80 per cent of Turkey's arms as the atrocities peaked by the mid-1990s. As a strategic ally and military outpost, Turkey had received a substantial flow of US arms throughout the post-World War II era. Arms transfers increased sharply in 1984, as Turkey initiated a military campaign against its miserably-oppressed Kurdish population. Military, police, and paramilitary operations increased in intensity and violence in the 1990s, along with atrocities and US arms and military training. Turkey set two records in 1994, correspondent Jonathan Randal observed: 1994 was "the year of the worst repression in the Kurdish provinces," and the year when Turkey became "the biggest single importer of American military hardware and thus the world's largest arms purchaser," including advanced armaments, "all of which were eventually used against the Kurds," along with extensive co-production and other co-operation with Turkey's military and its military industry. In the year 1997 alone, arms from the Clinton Administration surpassed the entire period from 1950 to 1983.[15]

Thanks to the steady supply of heavy armaments, military training, and diplomatic support, Turkey was able to crush Kurdish resistance, leaving tens of thousands killed, 2–3 million refugees, and 3,500 villages destroyed (seven times Kosovo under NATO bombing).

In this case, responsibility is easy to determine. Oppression of Kurds, and Turks who called for justice, has been outrageous since the founding of the modern Turkish state. The brutality of the counter-insurgency war has been amply recorded by highly credible sources. There is not the slightest question about the contribution of "the idealistic New World bent on ending inhumanity." Presumably, it is the impossibility of conjuring up a pretext of even minimal plausibility that accounts for the virtual suppression of these atrocities and Washington's role in implementing them.[16]

On the rare occasions when the matter breaks through the silence, the typical reaction is that the "American failure to protect Kurds in Turkey is inconsistent with its self-declared intention to protect Kosovars," in the words of Thomas Cushman. Or, according to Aryeh Neier, that the US "tolerated" the abuses suffered by the Kurds.[17] These regrettable lapses show that we are sometimes "inconsistent" and "look away" – because of the limits of our capacity to stop injustice, according to a common theme, articulated by the leader of the enlightened states in the manner quoted above.

Such reactions constitute a particularly sharp rejection of the moral truisms mentioned earlier: they are cynical apologetics for major atrocities for which one shares direct responsibility. There was no "looking away" in the case of Turkey and the Kurds: Washington "looked right there," as did its allies, saw what was happening, and acted decisively to intensify the atrocities, particularly during the Clinton years. The

US did not "fail to protect the Kurds" or "tolerate" the abuses they suffered, any more than Russia "fails to protect" the people of Grozny or "tolerates" their suffering. The new generation drew the line by consciously putting as many guns as possible into the hands of the killers and torturers – not just guns, but jet planes, tanks, helicopter gunships, all the most advanced instruments of terror – sometimes in secret, because arms were sent in violation of congressional legislation.

At no point was there any defensive purpose, nor any relation to the Cold War. That should come as no surprise: much the same has been true elsewhere as well through the Cold War years. This we learn from close attention to the historical events and internal planning record, though great power confrontations were always in the background and provided useful pretexts for the resort to force, terror and economic warfare. Furthermore, the charge of "inconsistency" requires proof, not mere assertion: it is necessary to demonstrate, not merely proclaim, that other actions are humanitarian in intent, a posture that accompanies virtually every resort to force throughout history.

A more realistic interpretation is given by Tim Judah in his account of the conflict in Kosovo: "Western countries may well sympathize with the plight of the Kurds or Tibetans," or the victims of Russian bombing in Chechnya, "but *realpolitik* means that there is little they are willing, or able, to do to help them."[18] In the case of Tibetans and Chechens, helping them might lead to a major war. In the case of the Kurds, helping them would interfere with US power interests. Accordingly, we cannot help them but must rather join in perpetrating atrocities against them; and responsible intellectuals must keep the truth hidden under a veil of silence, apologetics, and deceit while hailing their leaders, and themselves, for their unique devotion to "principles and values."

One of the regions most devastated by the US – Turkish assault was Tunceli, north of the Kurdish capital of Dyirbakir, where one-third of the villages were destroyed and vast tracts were set aflame by US-supplied helicopters and jets. "The terror in Tunceli is state terror," a Turkish minister conceded in 1994, reporting that village burning and terror had already driven 2 million people from their homes, left without even a tent to protect them. On April 1 2000, 10,000 Turkish troops began a new sweep of the area, while 5–7,000 troops with helicopter gunships crossed into Iraq to attack Kurds there once again – in a "no-fly zone," where Kurds are protected by the US Air force from the (temporarily) wrong oppressor.[19]

Recall that in Serbia, NATO was "fighting because no decent person can stand by and watch the systematic state-directed murder of other people," as Vaclav Havel puts it. While, according to Tony Blair, the "new generation" of leaders was enforcing "a new internationalism where the brutal repression of whole ethnic groups will no longer be tolerated" and "those responsible for such crimes have nowhere to hide." And, in the words of President Clinton, "If somebody comes after innocent civilians and tries to kill them en masse because of their race, their ethnic background or their religion, and it's within our power to stop it, we will stop it." But it is not within our power to stop our own enthusiastic participation in "systematic state-directed murder" and "brutal repression of whole ethnic groups," and those responsible for such crimes have no need to hide; rather, they enjoy the accolades of the educated classes, who marvel at the "saintly glow" of their deeds and the high ideals that inspire them.

Furthermore, "decent people" are expected to understand that NATO powers are not only entitled to oppress and terrorize their own populations, with our lavish assistance, but also to invade other countries at will. The same prerogative extends to non-NATO client states, notably Israel, which occupied South Lebanon for twenty-two years in violation of Security Council orders, but with US authorization and assistance, and during those years killed tens of thousands of people, repeatedly driving hundreds of thousands from their homes and destroying civilian infrastructure, again in early 2000 – always with US support and arms. Virtually none of this had to do with self-defense, as is well recognized within Israel and by human rights organizations, though different stories are preferred in the US information system.[20]

In June 2000, Israel did at last withdraw from Lebanon, or more accurately, was driven out by Lebanese resistance. The UN General Assembly voted to provide almost $150 million for UN (UNIFIL) monitors to ensure security in southern Lebanon and facilitate reconstruction of the devastated region. The resolution passed 110–2. The US and Israel voted against it because it also called upon Israel to pay the UN some $1.28 million in compensation for its attack on a UN compound, killing over 100 civilians who had taken refuge there, during its 1996 invasion of Lebanon.[21]

The achievements of Western terror are highly regarded. Just as Turkey was launching new military campaigns in its south-east region and across the border on April 1 2000, Secretary of Defense William Cohen addressed the American–Turkish Council Conference in a festive event with much laughter and applause. He praised Turkey for taking part in the humanitarian bombing of Serbia and announced that Turkey would participate in developing the Pentagon's advanced Joint Strike fighter, just as it was co-producing the F-16s that it has been using to such good effect in approved forms of ethnic cleansing and other atrocities – within NATO, not near its borders. "This is an exciting time to really not only be alive, but to be in positions of public service," Cohen continued, as "we have entered, with the turn of the century, a brave new world" with "so much creative opportunity out there that all of us can take advantage of," symbolized by the US–Turkey jet fighter project that will "put Turkey in the forefront and leadership of building a secure and stable Middle East" along with its close Israeli ally.

Shortly after, the State Department released its "latest annual report describing the administration's efforts to combat terrorism," Judith Miller reported. The report singled out Turkey for praise for its "positive experiences" in showing how "tough counter-terrorism measures plus political dialogue with non-terrorist opposition groups" can overcome the plague of violence and atrocities, reported without a trace of embarrassment.[22]

The first case study strongly confirms the evaluation of the new era by the skeptics. Perhaps it even gives some insight into the "moral purpose" that inspires us: "A gross injustice had been done to people, right on the doorstep of the European Union, which we were in a position to prevent and reverse, and we had to do that," in the words of Tony Blair.[23] Blair is not referring to righteous terror and ethnic cleansing that his government and its allies help to implement within NATO, but rather the atrocities that were being carried out by an official enemy, under NATO's bombs.

In 1999, Turkey relinquished its position as the leading recipient of US military aid, replaced by Colombia.[24] We therefore have a second natural case study for the inquiry into the alternative evaluations of the new era.

Colombia has had the worst human rights record in the Western hemisphere through the 1990s and has also been the hemisphere's leading beneficiary of US military aid and training, a longstanding correlation.[25] Colombia receives more than the rest of Latin America and the Caribbean combined, with a threefold increase from 1998 to 1999. The total is scheduled to increase sharply with the US contribution to the $7.5 billion "Plan Colombia," attributed to Bogota though "with heavy coaching from the Americans," as the *Wall Street Journal* puts it; according to non-US diplomats, the Plan was written in English. Plan Colombia calls for the US to provide over $1 billion in military aid, while others are to fund social, economic, and human rights programs. The military component was put in place during 1999, extending earlier programs; the rest is in abeyance.[26]

The shift in rank reflects the fact that Turkey's ethnic cleansing operations and other atrocities through the 1990s largely succeeded, at severe human cost; while state terror in Washington's client state of Colombia is still far from having achieved its goals, despite some 3,000 political murders and 300,000 refugees a year, the total by now perhaps approaching

2 million, the third largest population of displaced people in the world after Sudan and Angola. A political party outside the traditional elite power-sharing arrangement was permitted to function in 1985. It was soon "annihilated," with over 3,500 members "murdered or disappeared,"[27] including presidential candidates, mayors, and others, a feat accomplished without tarnishing Colombia's democratic credentials in Washington.

The overwhelming mass of atrocities are attributed to paramilitaries, who are closely linked to the military that receives US aid and training, all heavily involved in narco-trafficking. According to the Colombian government and leading human rights groups (the Colombian Commission of Jurists and others), the rate of killings increased by almost 20 per cent in 1999 and the proportion attributed to the paramilitaries rose from 46 per cent in 1995 to almost 80 per cent in 1998, continuing through 1999. The State Department confirms the general picture in its annual human rights reports. Its report covering 1999 concludes that "security forces actively collaborated with members of paramilitary groups" while "Government forces continued to commit numerous, serious abuses, including extrajudicial killings, at a level that was roughly similar to that of 1998," when the Department attributed to the military and paramilitaries about 80 per cent of atrocities with an identifiable source.

Massacres reached over one a day in early 1999 as Colombia displaced Turkey as the leading recipient of US arms. In June–August 1999, 200,000 more people were driven from their homes, according to Colombian and international human rights organizations.

The escalating US military aid is under the pretext of a drug war that is taken seriously by few competent observers, for substantial reasons. Quite apart from the matter of plausibility, it is noteworthy that the pretext is based on the remarkable presupposition, virtually unquestioned, that the US has the right to carry out military actions and chemical and biological warfare in other countries to eradicate a crop it does not like, though presumably "modern notions of justice" do not entitle Colombia – or Thailand, or China, or many others – to do the same in North Carolina, to eliminate a far more lethal drug, which they have been compelled to accept (along with advertising) under threat of trade sanctions, at a cost of millions of lives.

The second case study leads to the same conclusion as the first: the new era is much like earlier ones, including the familiar "cloak of moralistic righteousness."

Let us turn to a third example, perhaps the most obvious test case for evaluating the conflicting interpretations of the new era.

While Colombia replaced Turkey as leading recipient of US military aid, and the US and Britain were preparing to bomb Serbia in pursuit of their moral purpose, important events were underway in another part of the world, the scene of one of the worst human rights catastrophes of the late twentieth century: East Timor, which in 1999 was subjected to new atrocities, so extreme that they came to rank alongside of Kosovo in the concerns of the new era for human rights, humanitarian intervention, and limits of sovereignty.

The modern tragedy of East Timor has unfolded since December 1975, when Indonesia invaded and occupied the former Portuguese colony after it had declared independence, later annexing it. The invasion led to the slaughter of some 200,000 people, almost one-third of the population, and vast destruction, torture, and terror, renewed once again in 1999. To determine how the second major example of 1999 bears on the conflicting interpretations of the new era, we want to determine what has taken place, and how it is depicted. I will keep here to a summary, returning to a closer look in chapter 2.

The events of 1999 are reviewed in the January 2000 issue of the *American Journal of International Law*, offering the standard Western version: that the atrocities in East Timor took place six months after Kosovo – that is, after the August 30 1999 referendum on independence – but that:

> Unlike the case of Kosovo, which preceded the events in East Timor by six months, no state (including the United States) advocated a forcible military intervention in East Timor. The apparent reasons for this reluctance were that Indonesia possessed a strong military, that such an intervention was likely to be strongly opposed by nearby China, and that concerned states believed that Indonesia's consent to a multinational force would, in any case, soon be forthcoming.[28]

The account is indeed standard. To select another example virtually at random, consider William Shawcross's recent study of the interaction of the three "benign forces" in the world – the UN, the NGOs, and the liberal democracies – and the "malign force" of "warlords who have dominated the 1990s," Saddam Hussein and Slobodan Milosevic being "the two who stand out."[29] Some places were "bathed by the light of the West's concern – Bosnia and Kosovo, for example," though "others were obscured by our lack of interest." The book ends with a chapter entitled "From Kosovo to East Timor," reflecting the perceived order of events in these two major crises of 1999: "in both cases the international community was forced to confront a humanitarian disaster which was in part the product of its own neglect, and had to decide what price it was prepared to pay to right it."

Many commentators have described the intervention in Kosovo as a precedent for the dispatch of peacekeeping forces to East Timor. Hence even critics of the NATO bombing agree that it had benign effects. Others point out that "the United States does not want to be a 'globocop' now any more than it did in the past, sacrificing American resources and lives to the East Timors of the world," as when a UN peacekeeping force entered "Indonesian territory . . . to stop the killing" at US initiative.[30]

Virtually none of this is tenable. The truth of the matter, readily established, tells us a good deal about the norms of conduct that are likely to prevail if self-serving doctrine remains immune to critical reflection, and moral truisms are kept at the margins of consciousness.

The humanitarian catastrophe in East Timor was not "the product of [the] neglect" of the liberal democracies. It was substantially their creation, as in the previous cases discussed. When invading East Timor in 1975, Indonesia relied almost entirely on US arms and diplomatic support, renewed as atrocities reached near-genocidal levels in 1978 and persisting as violent oppression took its toll at the hands of a criminal who ranks high among the elite of Shawcross's "malign force," and was routinely praised as a "moderate" who is "at heart benign" – "our kind of guy," in the words of the Clinton Administration – until he lost control in 1997 and had to be discarded. In 1978, as Suharto's slaughter in East Timor peaked in fury, the US was joined by Britain, along with France and other powers. US–British support and participation continued through the escalating humanitarian catastrophe of 1999 and its consummation after the August 30 referendum on independence. East Timor was "Indonesian territory" only in that leaders of the liberal democracies effectively authorized the conquest in violation of Security Council directives and a World Court ruling.

The order of events in the standard version is crucially reversed. The latest wave of atrocities in East Timor was underway from November 1998. Well before the referendum on independence, atrocities in 1999 alone had reached levels beyond Kosovo prior to the NATO bombing, the relevant standard of comparison. Furthermore, ample public information was available indicating that much worse was to come unless the population submitted to Indonesian terror, and far more was known to Australian and surely US intelligence. Nonetheless, the new generation continued to provide military aid, even to conduct joint military exercises just prior to the referendum, while opposing any move to deter the further atrocities they had every reason to expect. Even after the August 30 referendum, the US insisted that Indonesia must remain in control of the illegally occupied territory while its forces virtually destroyed the country and drove 750,000 people – 85 per cent of the population – out of their homes.

Whatever one thinks of Kosovo, it could not have served as a precedent for humanitarian intervention in East Timor because of the timing alone; and more fundamentally, because humanitarian intervention never took place. There was, in fact, no "intervention" at all in any serious sense of the term, nor could there have been, if only because there was no question of sovereignty. Even Australia, the one Western country to have granted explicit *de jure* recognition to the Indonesian annexation (in large measure because of its interest in joint exploitation of Timorese oil), had renounced that stand in January 1999. Indonesia's sovereign rights were comparable to those of Nazi Germany in occupied Europe. They rested solely on great power ratification of aggression and massacre in this Portuguese-administered territory, a UN responsibility. The Russian drive to the West during World War II and the Normandy landing were not interventions; *a fortiori*, the entry of Australian-led UN peacekeeping forces after the Indonesian army withdrew does not qualify as intervention. The issue of humanitarian intervention does not even arise, though this is one of the rare cases when it is possible to speak seriously of humanitarian intent, at least on the part of Australia, or, more accurately, its population, who were bitterly critical of their government's failure to act as the toll of victims mounted from early 1999.

One element of the standard version is correct: no state advocated military intervention – reasonably enough, since there is little reason to suppose that any form of "intervention" would have been needed to terminate the atrocities, either those of 1999 or of the preceding decades of horror. There was no need to impose sanctions or to bomb Jakarta. Even the hint of withdrawal of participation in mid-September 1999 sufficed to make it clear to the Indonesian generals that the game was over. The result could very likely have been achieved in similar ways long before, had there been any willingness to interfere with the exploits of the "malign force" who was so ably serving the interests of Western power and privilege.

The standard reasons put forth to distinguish Kosovo from East Timor, just quoted, are not very convincing. Serbia "possessed a strong military," the main reason why invasion was never contemplated and bombers kept to a safe distance. More important, Indonesia's army, unlike that of Serbia, is heavily dependent on the United States, as was revealed in mid-September 1999, when Clinton finally give the signal to desist. Russia strongly opposed the NATO bombing, but that did not deter the US and its allies. Prior to mid-September, there was no expectation that Indonesia would "consent to a multinational force," if only because the "concerned states" had evinced no serious interest in this outcome (and Indonesia firmly rejected it). The main opponent of even unarmed "intervention" in the earlier months of rising terror had been Washington, and its opposition persisted at the height of the post-referendum atrocities.

Washington's principles were outlined succinctly by the highly regarded Australian diplomat Richard Butler, who transmitted to his fellow countrymen what he had learned from "senior American analysts": the US will act in its own perceived interest; others are to shoulder the burdens and face the costs, unless some power interest is served.[31] That seems a fair rendition of the reality of the new era of enlightenment and high principle, as the case of East Timor dramatically illustrates, adding another informative case study to the list.

One of the leading principles of the new era is that sovereignty may now be disregarded in the interest of defending human rights; disregarded by the "enlightened states," that is, not by others. Thus, the US and Britain accord themselves the right to carry out military and economic warfare with the alleged intent of containing Saddam Hussein, but there is no thought of endorsing an Iranian invasion of Iraq to overthrow the tyrant, though Iran suffered grievously from the Iraqi invasion of Iran, backed by the US and Britain, among others. The proclaimed principle has merit, or would, if it were upheld in a way that honest people could take seriously. The restriction of agents already undercuts that possibility. The two prime examples brought forth in 1999 suffice to eliminate any further illusions.

Indonesia's non-existent claim to sovereignty in East Timor was accorded the most delicate respect under the operative principles of the enlightened states. They insisted that its military forces must be assigned responsibility for security while they were conducting yet another reign of terror. As for Kosovo, the US and its allies require that it must remain under Serbian sovereignty, probably out of fear of a "greater Albania." But the sovereignty that NATO insists upon in Serbia is "trumped" by its claim that it is defending human rights, unlike East Timor, where non-sovereignty "trumps" any concern for the human rights that the leaders of NATO are brutally violating.

The new era is a dazzling one indeed.

The realities that Richard Butler described were well illustrated in East Timor in April 1999, the peak moment of exuberance about the new era. By then massacres organized by the troops armed and trained by the US and Britain were a regular occurrence, some extraordinary, extensively reported in Australia particularly. On August 6 – by coincidence the day of the report on the new Clinton Doctrine with its commitment "to stop" the killing of "innocent civilians" if "it's within our power" to do so – the Church in East Timor reported that 3–5,000 people had been killed so far in 1999, about twice the number killed on all sides in Kosovo in the year before the NATO bombing, according to NATO. And under very different circumstances. The East Timorese victims of Western-supported Indonesian aggression were defenseless civilians. There was no active fighting, no takeover of substantial territory by foreign-based guerrillas, no attacks on police and civilians with the avowed goal of eliciting violent retaliation that would lead to Western military intervention. The small resistance forces were confined to isolated mountain areas with virtually no international contact, and the atrocities were almost entirely attributable to the occupying army and its paramilitary associates, and of course to their foreign backers, primarily the US and Britain, as had been true for twenty-four years. The situation in Kosovo, to which we turn in chapter 3, was different in all of these respects.

In East Timor in 1999, the principles and values of the enlightened states dictated the same conclusion as in Turkey and in Colombia, where massacres had reached over one a day: support the killers. There was also one reported massacre in Kosovo, at Racak on January 15 (forty-five killed). That event allegedly inspired such horror among Western humanitarians that it was necessary to bomb Yugoslavia ten weeks later with the expectation, quickly fulfilled, that the consequence might be a sharp escalation of atrocities.[32]

These examples constitute only a partial sample of the circumstances that evoked the remarkable chorus of self-congratulation about the new era in which Western leaders devote themselves to their "moral purpose" in the name of "the international community" – which objects, strenuously and irrelevantly. Putting aside the actual facts about Kosovo, the performance was greatly facilitated by silence or deceit about what would have been highlighted at the same time, if the moral truisms mentioned at the outset could be entertained.

The test cases most directly relevant to the conflicting evaluations of the new era are those just briefly reviewed: major atrocities of the current period that could have easily been mitigated or terminated merely by withdrawal of direct and decisive participation – or in the terminology favored by apologists for state violence, atrocities that the US "tolerated" while "failing to protect" the victims. The preferred test cases, however, are Chechnya, Tibet, and others that have the advantage that the current phase of the crimes can be attributed to others. The only questions that arise have to do with our reaction to the other fellow's crimes, a far more comfortable stance.

The most extreme examples of this category are the African wars. Putting aside highly relevant history, the atrocities are not directly sponsored by the new generation, as in the examples reviewed. Here Washington's attitude is very much as outlined by National Security Adviser Sandy Berger and diplomat Richard Butler: there is no perceived gain in assisting the victims of terror, so there is no need to respond (except by sending arms to fuel the conflicts). As plans to bomb Serbia were reaching their final stages in February 1999, Western diplomats described Clinton's policies in Africa as "leaving Africa to solve its own crises." European and UN diplomats reported that "the United States has actively thwarted efforts by the United Nations to take on peacekeeping operations that might have prevented some of Africa's wars." In the Congo, Clinton's refusal to provide trivial sums for UN peacekeepers "torpedoed" the UN proposal, according to the UN's senior Africa envoy. Sierra Leone is a striking example. In 1997, "Washington dragged out discussions on a British proposal to deploy peacekeepers," then did nothing in the face of mounting horrors. In May 2000, UN Secretary-General Kofi Annan called for military support for the UN peacekeeping forces that were unable to contain the atrocities. But US officials reported that "the Clinton administration would not budge from offering only logistical and technical support," which turned out to be a fraud. Clinton offered US planes, but only for an exorbitant fee. "When Washington offers support equipment, like planes to fly in other countries' troops, 'the US offers are usually three times the commercial rate'," Annan said, and "Washington will not put an American officer on the ground." It is difficult for the UN to afford even commercial rates because of the US refusal to pay its debt.[33]

Again the same conclusions. With a degree of clarity rare in international affairs, the evaluation of the new era by the skeptics wins hands down. Though without any possible effect, because of the impenetrable cocoon spun by responsible intellectuals: at worst, we "tolerate" the crimes of others, and we may then proceed to castigate ourselves for failing to react properly to them, thereby revealing our commitment to high moral principles and willingness to acknowledge even our most serious flaws.

While elementary considerations suffice to put to rest the triumphalism that accompanied the bombing of Serbia, nonetheless the question of why the decision was made to go to war remains open, as does the question of its legitimacy. It remains possible that there really is an "inconsistency," though not of the kind discussed in the apologetic literature: it is possible that in the special case of Kosovo, the new generation was violating standard operating procedure and acting with a "moral purpose," as claimed – with considerable passion, but little detectable argument.

As noted, the official justifications, which remained fairly constant throughout, were reiterated by Secretary of Defense William Cohen and Chairman of the Joint Chiefs Henry Shelton in January 2000: the primary motivating factors were:

1. "Ensuring the stability of Eastern Europe"
2. "Thwarting ethnic cleansing"
3. "Ensuring NATO's credibility"

though the second alone would not have sufficed, National Security Adviser Sandy Berger elaborated. "National interest" must be at stake, the first and third reasons.

The third reason is the one that has been most insistently advanced, and it has merit, when properly understood: "credibility of NATO" means "credibility of US power"; the "disorderly" elements of the world must understand the price they will pay if they do not heed the orders of the master in Washington.[34] The first reason – "ensuring stability" – also has plausibility, though again terms must be understood properly: not in their literal but in their doctrinal sense. Correctly understood, a region is "stable" if it is incorporated within the US-dominated global system with approved interests served and the right power centers in charge.

In the literal but not the doctrinal sense, Eastern Europe was mostly stable under Kremlin rule. In the doctrinal sense, the regions dominated by Jakarta became stable in 1965 when a military dictatorship was imposed after a Rwanda-style slaughter that destroyed the mass-based party of poor peasants, the PKI, which "had won widespread support not as a revolutionary party but as an organization defending the interests of the poor within the existing system," developing a "mass base among the peasantry" through its "vigor in defending the interests of the . . . poor." Concern that the PKI could not be blocked by "ordinary democratic means" was a primary reason for Washington's clandestine war aiming to dismantle Indonesia in 1958, and when that failed, support for the military, whose goal was "to exterminate the PKI."[35] For this reason, along with its pro-China stance, the PKI was a source of "instability." US–UK participation in subsequent atrocities of the perpetrators of the 1965 slaughter is understandable, given that Indonesia is "so central to the stability of the region," as explained once again in September 1999 as Indonesia's assaults mounted in ferocity.

Similarly, Washington had to impose a murderous military dictatorship in Guatemala because its first democratic government "has become an increasing threat to the stability of

Honduras and El Salvador," State Department officials warned. Stability in the doctrinal sense was threatened because Guatemala's "agrarian reform is a powerful propaganda weapon; its broad social program of aiding the workers and peasants in a victorious struggle against the upper classes and large foreign enterprises has a strong appeal to the populations of Central American neighbors where similar conditions prevail." After forty years of terror, there are no such programs, so Guatemala is not a threat to stability. In the doctrinal sense, it is even possible, without contradiction, to "destabilize" in order to bring "stability." Thus Nixon–Kissinger "efforts to destabilize a freely elected Marxist government in Chile" were undertaken because "we were determined to seek stability," a leading foreign affairs analyst observed.[36]

Understanding terms in their doctrinal sense, it is reasonable to suppose that "ensuring the stability of Eastern Europe" was a goal of the bombing, along with "ensuring NATO's credibility."

The second justification – "thwarting ethnic cleansing" – had little credibility during the war, and that little has diminished considerably in the light of extensive evidence that has since been provided by the US and other Western sources. Elaborating this second justification, Cohen and Shelton assert that prior to the bombing, "the Belgrade regime's cruel repression in Kosovo [had] created a humanitarian crisis of staggering proportions," and "Milosević's campaign, which he dubbed 'Operation Horseshoe', would have led to even more homelessness, starvation, and loss of life had his ruthlessness gone unchecked." Before the March 24 1999 bombing, Milosevic was "finalizing this barbaric plan," and on March 21, the day after the withdrawal of the Kosovo Verification Mission (KVM) monitors, Serb forces "launched a major offensive," "dubbed 'Operation Horseshoe'." Testifying before Congress a few months earlier, Cohen said that "now we know, in retrospect, that he had an Operation Horseshoe whereby he was determined he was going to carry out his objectives, and he believed that he could carry them out in a very short period of time, in a week or so," had the bombing not thwarted his plans.[37]

"Operation Horseshoe" has been adduced by many knowledgeable commentators as a justification for the bombing. To mention only one example, Brookings Institution senior fellows Ivo Daalder and Michael O'Hanlon, with experience in and out of government on Balkans-related issues, write that in late 1998, "Milosevic approved Operation Horseshoe – a plan of truly evil proportions designed to reengineer Kosovo by pushing much of its civilian population permanently out of the province." Therefore current "problems in Kosovo are nothing compared with what would have happened if NATO had not intervened."[38]

One fact is unquestioned: the NATO bombing was followed by a rapid escalation of atrocities and ethnic cleansing. But that, in itself, is a condemnation of the bombing, not a justification for it. As for the rest, the picture has several problems.

One problem is that the massive documentation provided by Washington, NATO, and other Western sources provides no meaningful evidence of a Serb offensive after the withdrawal of the monitors, though it provides rich evidence of Serb ethnic cleansing operations immediately after the bombing began. We return to this matter, noting, however, that even if a Serb offensive was launched after the withdrawal of the monitors in clear preparation for a military assault, that would hardly serve to justify their withdrawal over official Serbian objection (a fact not yet reported in the mainstream, though it was public knowledge the day before the bombing),[39] and the military attack that it effectively announced.

Another problem has to do with the distinction between plans and implementation. The contingency plans of the great powers and their clients, insofar as they are known, are horrendous; those that are unknown are doubtless worse.[40] That Milosevic had plans "of truly evil proportions" for Kosovo has scarcely been in doubt, even without access to internal records, just as it is a near certainty that Israel has plans to expel much of the Palestinian population, and if under serious threat of bombing and invasion by Iran or Syria, would be preparing to carry them out. It is also hardly in doubt that in March 1999, under constant and highly credible threats of bombing and invasion by the reigning superpower and the military alliance it dominates, Serbian military forces were preparing to carry out such plans in Kosovo. But it is a long step from the existence of plans and preparation to the conclusion that the plans will be implemented unless the planner is subjected to military attack – eliciting the implementation of the plans, which retrospectively justifies the attack by an impressive feat of logic.

It is appropriate to be "in no doubt that the ethnic cleansing was systematically planned before the NATO bombing"; it would be astonishing if that were not true, under the circumstances. But evidence is required to support the statement that

"Western intelligence confirms [ethnic cleansing] was already underway before the first NATO airstrikes" – and before the withdrawal of the monitors, if the evidence is to have any force.[41] It is also necessary to account for Washington's inability to make the evidence public in the extensive documentation it has released, to which we return.

Further questions arise with regard to "Operation Horseshoe," allegedly discovered by German authorities two weeks after the bombing began and known only "in retrospect," according to Secretary of Defense Cohen, hence not a motive for the bombing. Curiously, the plan was kept secret from NATO Commanding General Wesley Clark, who, when asked about Operation Horseshoe a month after the bombing began, informed the press that plans for it "have never been shared with me."[42] Retired German general Heinz Loquai, who works for the Organisation for Security and Co-operation in Europe (OSCE), alleges in a new book that "the plan was fabricated from run-of-the-mill Bulgarian intelligence reports," and has "come to the conclusion that no such operation ever existed." According to the German news weekly *Die Woche*, the alleged plan was "a general analysis by a Bulgarian intelligence agency of Serbian behaviour in the war." The journal reports further that "maps broadcast around the world as proof of NATO's information were drawn up at the German defence headquarters," and that the Bulgarian report "concluded that the goal of the Serbian military was to destroy the Kosovo Liberation Army, and not to expel the entire Albanian population, as was later argued by [German Defence Minister Rudolf] Scharping and the Nato leadership." Loquai claims further that the German defense ministry "even coined the name 'Horseshoe'." He also notes "a fundamental flaw in the German account: it named the operation 'Potkova', which is the Croatian word for horseshoe," instead of using the Serbian word "Potkovica." Loquai's book was favorably received in the German press, which also criticized Scharping's "propaganda lies" (eg, doubling the alleged number of Serbian troops prior to the bombing from 20,000 to 40,000) and his evasion of the charges.[43]

Yet another problem is that General Clark also had no knowledge of any plan to "thwart ethnic cleansing." When the bombing began on March 24, he informed the press – repeatedly, insistently, forcefully – that brutal Serb atrocities would be an "entirely predictable" consequence of the bombing, later elaborating that NATO military operations were not designed to block "Serb ethnic cleansing" or even to wage war against Serbian forces in Kosovo. US government and other sources available at the time lent considerable plausibility to Clark's judgment. Substantial documentation has been released since by the State Department, NATO, the KVM, the OSCE, and other Western and independent sources, much of it produced in an effort to justify NATO's war. We return to all of this in chapter 3, merely noting here that it strongly confirms General Clark's analysis, to an extent I found surprising. Even more surprising, the documentation lends little support to the belief that atrocities mounted significantly after withdrawal of the KVM monitors on March 20, contrary to what seemed to me a natural expectation at the time.

The conclusions about the anticipated effects of NATO's policy choices do not comport well with the stance of nobility.

Accordingly, the preferred account during the bombing, repeated endlessly since, is that its objective was "to stem Belgrade's expulsion of ethnic Albanians from Kosovo" under Operation Horseshoe – the expulsion apparently precipitated by the bombing (or its virtual announcement, according to the Secretary of Defense, contrary to Washington's official record to which we return), and an objective unknown to the military commander and forcefully denied by him, just as he was unaware of Operation Horseshoe. Similarly, critics of the air war as ineffectual conclude "that air power failed to prevent the very ethnic cleansing that prompted Western leaders to act in the first place," a reversal of the chronological order of events; at least that much seems reasonably clear, whatever one's judgment about the actions undertaken. In a widely praised book on the war, historian David Fromkin asserts without argument that the US and its allies acted out of "altruism" and "moral fervor" alone, forging "a new kind of approach to the use of power in world politics," as they "reacted to the deportation of more than a million Kosovars from their homeland" by bombing so as to save them "from horrors of suffering, or from death." He is referring to those expelled as the anticipated consequence of the bombing. International affairs and security specialist Alan Kuperman writes that in East Timor and Kosovo, "the threat of economic sanctions or bombing has provoked a tragic backlash," and "Western intervention arrived too late to prevent the widespread atrocities." In Kosovo, the threat of bombing did not arrive "too late to prevent the widespread atrocities," but preceded them, as did the bombing itself if official documents are to be believed. In East Timor, no Western action "provoked a tragic backlash." The use of force was not proposed, and even the threat of sanctions was delayed until after the consummation of the atrocities; and there was no "Western intervention" in any significant sense of the term.[44]

We are left with two plausible justifications for the bombing: ensuring "stability" and "the credibility of NATO," both understood in the doctrinal sense.

The surviving official reasons will plainly not do as support for the thesis that the new generation was pursuing a "moral purpose" in the case of Kosovo, let alone the more visionary theses about the new era. Therefore other arguments have been sought. One, noted earlier, is that the war served as a precedent for "humanitarian intervention" in East Timor six months later. Even if correct, that would not justify the bombing, plainly, but since the conclusion has no basis, the question is academic.

A common current version of Western motives for the 1999 bombing of Serbia is that the West was shamed by its failure to act in Bosnia. NATO chose to bomb, Fouad Ajami asserts,

against the advice of the pollsters and realists and believers in the primacy of "geoeconomics," to prosecute a just war, pulled into Kosovo as they had earlier been into Bosnia by the shame of what they had witnessed, by the image of themselves they had seen in that Balkan mirror.

According to Aryeh Neier, what "inspired the advocates of humanitarian intervention" in Kosovo was that "many persons in and out of government were determined not to allow a repetition in Kosovo" of what had happened in Bosnia.[45]

These claims are presented without argument as self-evident truths, following the norm for justification for state violence. The claims reject the official reasons offered at the time or since. That aside, though offered in justification of "the advocates of humanitarian intervention" in Kosovo, these claims are, in fact, a severe indictment of them, and of Western political and moral culture generally. According to this account, in radical violation of moral truisms the West is shamed by its image in the "Balkan mirror," where it is guilty only of inadequate response to the crimes of others, but not by its image in other mirrors, where the crimes trace right back home: those discussed earlier for example, where the West did not "tolerate" atrocities as Neier and others prefer to see it, but participated actively in escalating them. Furthermore, on this interpretation, while the guiding principles and values call for determination not to allow a repetition of crimes committed by an official enemy, they say nothing about repetition of our own comparable or worse crimes, and thus free the agents of "humanitarian intervention" and the "many persons" who support them from any concern over these, even recollection of them.

Because of the pairing of Kosovo and East Timor in public discourse in 1999, the latter offers a particularly striking illustration of these conclusions. It should therefore be stressed that the huge slaughter of earlier years in East Timor is (at least) comparable to the terrible atrocities that can plausibly be attributed to Milosevic in the earlier wars in Yugoslavia, and responsibility is far easier to assign, with no complicating factors. If proponents of the "repetition of Bosnia" thesis intend it seriously, they should certainly have been calling for bombing of Jakarta – indeed

Washington and London – in early 1999 so as "not to allow a repetition in East Timor" of the crimes that Indonesia, the US, and UK had perpetrated there for a quarter-century. And when the new generation of leaders refused to pursue this honorable course, they should have been leading honest citizens to do so themselves, perhaps joining the Bin Laden network. These conclusions follow straightforwardly, if we assume that the thesis is intended as something more than apologetics for state violence.

Quite apart from the startling self-indictment, and the lack of even a pretense of evidence, the argument must be one of the most remarkable justifications for state violence on record. According to this doctrine, military force is legitimate if failure to apply it might induce the target of the attack to carry out autrocities (as it did, as anticipated, after the attack and presumably in response to it). By that standard, violent states are free to act as they like, with the acclaim of the educated classes.

Another device for evading the consequences of "advocacy of humanitarian intervention" in Kosovo is to hold that NATO should have invaded outright, not bombed. That is easy to say, and could be taken seriously if accompanied by a reasoned proposal, at the time or since, taking account of the likely consequences of invasion (particularly in the light of US military doctrine), quite aside from non-trivial logistic and other problems.[46] One will search in vain for that, clearly the minimum that is required to meet the heavy burden of proof that must be borne, always, by advocates of the use of force, whatever the alleged intent.

Another useful mode of justification is to invent and refute absurd arguments against the bombing, while ignoring those actually presented. A favorite target is the argument, attributed to unnamed "leftists" or "revisionists," that the US has no right to intervene because of its disgraceful record. That the record of a state should be taken into account in considering the right of intervention is another truism, accepted by everyone who even pretends to be serious. But the argument that a disgraceful record automatically rescinds that right would be wholly irrational, hence easy to refute. This exercise can only be understood, once again, as a form of tacit recognition of inability to bear the burden of justification for the resort to violence – always heavy though not insuperable in principle, apart from dedicated pacifists.

The conclusion becomes even more clear when we inspect the occasional efforts to cite an actual source. This is rare, but there are a few examples. Thus, correspondent Ian Williams, who has compiled a distinguished record on other issues, writes that Edward Said and I "looked at the record of inaction by the West, in Palestine, East Timor, Kurdistan and so on, and therefore deduced that any action over Kosovo could not be for good motives and should therefore be opposed." To support the charge, and his ridicule of this "excessively theological attitude" and "moralizing element" that was "common to leftists across the spectrum," he cites nothing by Said and one statement of mine that says nothing even remotely relevant.[47] Even the most cursory reading of what I wrote makes it obvious, without the slightest doubt, that my position was exactly the opposite, even to the extent of reviewing the few examples of military intervention with benign consequences, hence arguably legitimate despite the ugly records of the agents. More striking is the way Williams falls so easily into the common mode of apologetics for state violence. Said and I did not look at the "record of inaction" of the West in the cases he mentions, but at the record of quite decisive *action*, a fact that evidently cannot be assimilated by many Western intellectuals. Again, the only reasonable conclusion is that the burden of justification cannot be met.

It takes considerable effort not to recognize the accuracy of the report to the UN Commission on Human Rights in March 2000 by former Czech dissident Jiri Dienstbier, now UN Special Investigator for the former Yugoslavia: "The bombing hasn't solved any problems," he reported: "It only multiplied the existing problems and created new ones." Or the corroborating assessment of Michael MccGwire that "while Serb forces were clearly the instrument of the unfolding 'humanitarian disaster', NATO's long-trailered urge to war was undoubtedly a primary cause," and reference to the "bombing as 'humanitarian intervention'" is "really grotesque":

> No one questions the underlying good intentions, but one suspects that much of the moralistic rhetoric, the demonizing, the claim to be pioneering a foreign policy based on values as well as interests, was a form of denial. It served to conceal from all of us the unpalatable fact that leaders and their people have to accept their share of the blame for unintended consequences – in this case the humanitarian disaster and the civilian casualties in Serbia,

which are, in fact, only part of the disaster.[48]

MccGwire's comments seem realistic, with qualifications about the matter of "intentions." The phrase "unintended consequences" obscures the fact that they were anticipated, even if they were not as "entirely predictable" as the NATO commander felt at the outset, in words that MccGwire quotes. Furthermore, it is far from true that "no one questions the underlying good intentions." They are most definitely questioned by those MccGwire calls "the world at large," as he emphasizes (see pp. 7–8). The conviction about unquestionable good intentions is particularly dubious against the background of the record of past and present practice, including the crucial test cases just reviewed in an effort to evaluate the conflicting interpretations of the new era.

Quite generally, it is hard to find significant inconsistency in the practices of the great powers, nor in the principles and values that actually guide policy. None of that should be in the least surprising to those who do not prefer what has sometimes been called "intentional ignorance."[49] We turn next to a closer examination of the two humanitarian catastrophes that have been adduced to ground the thesis of "moral purpose" and the vision of the future that has been constructed on that basis.

Notes

1. Tony Blair, in "A New Generation Draws the Line," *Newsweek*, April 19 1999; Vaclav Havel, "Kosovo and the End of the Nation-State," *New York Review*, June 10 1999.
2. Michael Wines, "Two Views of Inhumanity Split the World, Even in Victory," *New York Times Week in Review*, lead article, June 13 1999;

Michael Glennon, "The New Interventionism," *Foreign Affairs* (Council on Foreign Relations, New York), May/June 1999.

3. Bob Davis, "Cop of the World? Clinton Pledges U.S. Power Against Ethnic Cleansing, but His Aides Hedge," *Wall Street Journal* (henceforth *WSJ*), August 6 1999. William Jefferson Clinton, "A Just and Necessary War," *New York Times* (henceforth *NYT*), May 23; April 1, speech at Norfolk Air Station, *NYT*, April 2 1999.

4. Sebastian Mallaby, "Uneasy Partners," *NYT Book Review*, September 21 1997. Senior Administration policymaker cited by Thomas Friedman, *NYT*, January 12 1992. Davis, op. cit., paraphrasing Sandy Berger in an interview.

5. Department of Defense Report to Congress, *Kosovo/Operation Allied Force After-Action Report*, January 31 2000. Tony Blair, Alan Little, "Moral Combat: NATO At War," BBC2 Special, March 12 2000.

6. Declaration of Group of 77 South Summit, April 10–14 2000. For background, see *Third World Resurgence* (Penang), no. 117, 2000.

7. Anthony Sampson, "Mandela accuses 'policeman' Britain," *Guardian*, April 5 2000.

8. Schiff, Amnon Barzilai, *Ha'aretz*, April 5 2000. On Indian, Israeli, and Egyptian reactions, see my *The New Military Humanism: Lessons of Kosovo* (Monroe, ME: Common Courage, 1999), chapter 6; henceforth *NMH*.

9. On these events, see my *Deterring Democracy* (London, New York: Verso, 1991), and *NMH*.

10. Ibid. On Turkey and the Kurds, see *NMH*, and some comments below.

11. Andrew Kramer, "Putin following Yeltsin's misguided policies, Solzhenitsyn says," AP, *Boston Globe*, May 17 2000.

12. John Mearsheimer, "India Needs The Bomb," *NYT* op-ed, March 24 2000; Samuel Huntington, "The Lonely Superpower," *Foreign Affairs*, March/April 1999. Chalmers Johnson, *Blowback* (New York: Holt, 2000), 59. Michael MccGwire, "Why did we bomb Belgrade?" *International Affairs* (Royal Academy of International Affairs, London), 76.1, January 2000.

13. Christopher Marquis, "Bankrolling Colombia's War on Drugs," *NYT*, June 23 2000, last paragraph.

14. Tamar Gabelnick, William Hartung, and Jennifer Washburn, *Arming Repression: U.S. Arms Sales to Turkey During the Clinton Administration*

(New York and Washington: World Policy Institute and Federation of Atomic Scientists, October 1999). For further sources, see *NMH*. On Latin America and the Caribbean, see Adam Isacson and Joy Olson, *Just the Facts: 1999 Edition* (Washington: Latin America Working Group and Center for International Policy, 1999). Here and below, the perennial front-runners Israel and Egypt, which belong to a separate category, are excluded. Rankings are for fiscal years, and are qualitative, depending on exactly which aspects are counted (grants, sales, training, co-production, joint exercises, etc.).

15. See preceding note. Jonathan Randal, *After Such Knowledge, What Forgiveness: My Encounters with Kurdistan* (Boulder, CO: Westview 1999).

16. On the events and their refraction through doctrinal prisms, see *NMH*. For an update, my *Rogue States* (Cambridge MA: South End, 2000), chapter 5.

17. Thomas Cushman, editor, "Human Rights and the Responsibility of Intellectuals," *Human Rights Review*, January–March 2000; Aryeh Neier, "Inconvenient Facts," *Dissent*, spring 2000; in both cases, reaction to the review of US-backed Turkish atrocities in *NMH*.

18. Tim Judah, *Kosovo: War and Revenge* (New Haven: Yale University Press, 2000), 308.

19. Ferit Demer, Reuters, datelined Tunceli, Turkey, April 1; Chris Morris, *Guardian* (London), April 3 2000. AP, *Los Angeles Times*, April 2 2000.

20. See my *Fateful Triangle: US., Israel, and the Palestinians* (Cambridge MA: South End, 1999, updated from 1983 edition). The Lebanese government and international relief agencies report 25,000 killed since 1982; the toll of the 1982 invasion is estimated at about 20,000.

21. "Israel, US vote against funding for UN force in Lebanon," AP Worldstream, June 15; Marilyn Henry, "Israel, US angered by Kana clause in UN peacekeeping package," *Jerusalem Post*, June 18 2000. On the circumstances of the invasion, see *Fateful Triangle*. For detailed documentation, including the Amnesty International and UN inquiries that concluded that the shelling of the compound was intentional, see Shifra Stern, *Israel's Operation "Grapes of Wrath" and the Qana Massacre*, ms., April–May 1996.

22. Federal News Service, Department of Defense Briefing, Secretary William Cohen, "Turkey's Importance to 21st Century International

Security," Grand Hyatt Hotel, Washington DC, March 31; Charles Aldinger, "U.S. praises key NATO ally Turkey," Reuters, March 31 2000. Judith Miller, "South Asia Called Major Terror Hub in a Survey by U.S.," *NYT*, April 30 2000, lead story.

23. Little, op. cit.

24. See note 14.

25. See Lars Schoultz, *Comparative Politics*, January 1981; Schoultz is the author of the leading scholarly study of human rights and US policy in Latin America. For broader confirmation and inquiry, which helps explain the reasons, see the studies by economist Edward Herman reported in Chomsky and Herman, *Political Economy of Human Rights* (Boston: South End, 1979), vol. I. chapter 2.1.1, and Herman, *The Real Terror Network* (Boston: South End, 1982), 126ff. Note that these reviews precede the Reagan years, when inquiry would have been superfluous.

26. Carla Anne Robbins, "How Bogota Wooed Washington to Open New War on Cocaine," *WSJ*, June 23 2000. For sources on what follows, and further information and discussion, see *Rogue States*, chapter 5.

27. Rafael Pardo, "Colombia's Two-Front War," *Foreign Affairs* July/August 2000; Pardo was special government adviser on peace negotiations and Minister of Defense while the guerrilla-backed party was destroyed by assassination.

28. Sean Murphy, "Contemporary Practice of the United States Relating to International Law," *American Journal of International Law* (henceforth *AJIL*), 94.1, January 2000.

29. William Shawcross, *Deliver Us From Evil: Peacekeepers, Warlords and a World of Endless Conflict* (New York: Simon & Schuster, 2000), 26ff. Shawcross attributes this picture to US Deputy Secretary of State Strobe Talbott, but then adopts it with little qualification. In a critical review, *Wall Street Journal* editor Max Boot praises Shawcross for his "progress" in having come to understand that the US is a "benign force," after having sunk so low as to criticize "U.S. attacks on North Vietnamese bases in Cambodia" (the approved term for Cambodian civilians), *Foreign Affairs*, March/April 2000.

30. *Newsweek* diplomatic correspondent Michael Hirsh, "The Fall Guy," *Foreign Affairs*, November/December 1999.

31. Richard Butler, "East Timor: Principle v. Reality," *The Eye* (Australia), 7–20, 1999.

32. On the reporting of the Racak massacre, and the available evidence, see Edward Herman and David Peterson, "CNN: Selling Nato's War Globally," in Philip Hammond and Edward Herman, eds., *Degraded Capability: The Media and the Kosovo Crisis* (London: Pluto, 2000).

33. Colum Lynch, "US seen leaving Africa to solve its own crisis," *Boston Globe* (henceforth *BG*), February 19 1999. John Donnelly and Joe Lauria, "UN peace efforts on trial in Africa; Annan angry as U.S. holds to limits on military role," *BG*, May 11; Barbara Crossette, "U.N. Chief Faults Reluctance of U.S. To Help in Africa," *NYT*, May 13 2000.

34. On the notion of "credibility," and its nature and scope as understood by top planners and policy intellectuals, see *NMH*, chapter 6.

35. PKI success, Harold Crouch, *Army and Politics in Indonesia* (Ithaca, NY: Cornell University Press, 1978), 351, 155, a standard source. See next chapter, and sources cited.

36. Piero Gleijeses, *Shattered Hope* (Princeton, 1991), 365. *Foreign Affairs* editor James Chace, *NYT Magazine*, May 22 1977.

37. Note 5, above; William Cohen's testimony at the Hearing of the Senate Armed Services Committee on Kosovo operations, October 14 1999, Federal News Service.

38. Ivo Daalder and Michael O'Hanlon, "Without the air war, things could have been worse," *Washington Post National Weekly*, April 3 2000.

39. See *NMH*, 22, and chapter 3 below.

40. See *NMH*, chapter 6; and chapter 3 below.

41. Michael Ignatieff, "What is war for? And should we have done it?" *National Post* (Canada), April 18 2000; lengthy excerpts from his correspondence with Robert Skidelsky, taken from his book *Virtual War*.

42. "Panorama: War Room," BBC, April 19 1999.

43. John Goetz and Tom Walker, "Serbian ethnic cleansing scare was a fake, says general," *Sunday Times*, April 2 2000. Franziska Augstein, "Im Kosovo war es anders," *Frankfurter Allgemeine Zeitung*, March 25; also *Die Woche*, March 24; *Der Spiegel*, March 17; *Sueddeutsche Zeitung*, April 4; *Le Monde*, April 11 2000. Heinz Loquai, *Der Kosovo-Konflict: Wege in einen vermeidbaren Krieg* (Baden-Baden: Nomos Verlag, 2000).

44. Ruth Wedgwood, "NATO's Campaign in Yugoslavia," *AJIL*, 93.4, October 1999, a legal defense of the bombing. Donald Byman and

Matthew Waxman of Rand Corporation, "Kosovo and the Great Air Power Debate," *International Security*, 24.4, spring 2000. David Fromkin, *Kosovo Crossing* (Free Press, 1999); Alan Kuperman, "Rwanda in Retrospect," *Foreign Affairs*, January/February 2000. For many other examples, see *NMH* and chapter 3, below.

45. Fouad Ajami, "Wars and Rumors of War," *NYT Book Review*, June 11 2000; Aryeh Neier, op. cit., and many others. Neier's point is that it is "dishonest" for me (in *NMH*) to ignore this self-evident truth while keeping to the justifications that were actually put forth, and continue to be, as noted.

46. Testifying before the Defence Select Committee, Britain's second most senior defence minister during the war, Lord Gilbert, defence minister of state formally responsible for intelligence, ridiculed the suggestion that NATO could have invaded even by September 1999, informing the Committee that "a land invasion of Kosovo would have been possible by September, but by September this year [2000], not by September last year." Patrick Wintour, "War strategy ridiculed," *Guardian*, July 21 2000.

47. Ian Williams, "Left Behind: American Socialists, Human Rights, and Kosovo," *Human Rights Review*, 1–2, January–March 2000.

48. Jiri Dienstbier, BBC Summary of World Broadcasts, March 25; Naomi Koppel, "Ground Troops Urged for Yugoslavia," AP Online, March 29 2000; Elizabeth Sullivan, "A Threatening Thaw in the Balkans," *Cleveland Plain Dealer*, April 3; Laura Coffey, *Prague Post*, March 29 2000. MccGwire, op. cit. Dienstbier was a leading Czech dissident, imprisoned in the late 1970s and early 1980s, later the first post-Communist foreign minister.

49. Donald Fox and Michael Glennon, 'Report to the International Human Rights Law Group and the Washington Office on Latin America," Washington DC, April 1985, referring to State Department evasion of US-backed state terror in El Salvador.

CHAPTER TWO

"Green Light" for War Crimes

It is not easy to write with feigned calm and dispassion about the events that unfolded in East Timor in 1999. Horror and shame are compounded by the fact that the crimes are so familiar and could so easily have been terminated. That has been true ever since Indonesia invaded in December 1975, relying on US diplomatic support and arms – used illegally, but with secret authorization, even new arms shipments sent under the cover of an official embargo. There has been no need to threaten bombing or even sanctions. It would, very likely, have sufficed for the US and its allies to withdraw their participation, and to inform their close associates in the Indonesian military command that the atrocities must be terminated and the territory granted the right of self-determination that has been upheld by the United Nations and the International Court of Justice. We cannot undo the past, but should at least be willing to recognize what we have done, and to face the moral responsibility of saving the remnants and providing ample reparations, a pathetic gesture of compensation for terrible crimes.

The latest chapter in this painful story of betrayal and complicity opened after the referendum of 30 August 1999, when the population voted overwhelmingly for independence. Atrocities mounted sharply, organized and directed by the Indonesian military (TNI). A UN Security Council Mission gave its appraisal on September 11:

> The evidence for a direct link between the militia and the military is beyond any dispute and has been overwhelmingly documented by UNAMET [The UN Assistance Mission] over the last four months. But the scale and thoroughness of the destruction of East Timor in the past week has demonstrated a new level of open participation of the military in the implementation of what was previously a more veiled operation.

The Mission warned that "the worst may be yet to come . . . It cannot be ruled out that these are the first stages of a genocidal campaign to stamp out the East Timorese problem by force."[1]

Indonesia historian John Roosa, an official observer of the vote, described the situation starkly:

> Given that the pogrom was so predictable, it was easily preventable . . . But in the weeks before the ballot, the Clinton Administration refused to discuss with Australia and other countries the formation of [an international force]. Even after the violence erupted, the Administration dithered for days,[2]

until compelled by international (primarily Australian) and domestic pressure to make some timid gestures, threats to veto loans and cancellation of military co-operation – which was "quietly resumed" a few months later, "without fanfare to avoid criticism on Capitol Hill and among human rights groups."[3] These limited measures sufficed to induce the Indonesian generals to reverse course at once and to accept an international presence, illustrating the latent power that has always been at hand, overwhelmingly so since Indonesia's economic collapse in 1997.

The events of 1999 should evoke bitter memories. They were a shameful replay of events of twenty years earlier. After carrying out a huge slaughter in 1977–78 with the support of the Carter Administration, the regime of General Suharto felt confident enough to permit a brief visit by members of the Jakarta diplomatic corps, among them US Ambassador Edward Masters. The ambassadors and the journalists who accompanied them could see that an enormous humanitarian catastrophe had been created, reminiscent of Biafra and Cambodia. The aftermath was described by the distinguished Indonesia scholar Benedict Anderson: "For nine long months" of starvation and terror, Anderson testified at the United Nations, "Ambassador Masters deliberately refrained, even within the walls of the State Department, from proposing humanitarian aid to East Timor," waiting "until the generals in Jakarta gave him the green light" – until they felt "secure enough to permit foreign visitors," as an internal State Department document recorded. Only then did Washington consider taking some steps to deal with the consequence of its actions.[4]

While Clinton followed suit from February through August of 1999, the Indonesian military implemented a scarcely veiled campaign of terror and intimidation that has killed thousands of people according to the Church and other credible sources. And as he "dithered" in the final weeks, most of the population were expelled from their homes with unknown numbers killed and much of the country destroyed. According to UN figures, the TNI–paramilitary campaign "drove an estimated 750,000 of East Timor's 880,000 people from their homes," probably some 250,000 to Indonesian West Timor; elsewhere too, according to many reports, though no one is investigating. It is estimated that about 70 per cent of the country was levelled. More than 10,000 might have been killed, according to Bishop Carlos Felipe Ximenes Belo, 1996 Nobel Peace laureate, who was driven from the country under a hail of bullets, his house burned and gutted, and the refugees sheltering there dispatched to an uncertain fate.[5]

The air force that was able to carry out pin-point destruction of civilian targets in Novi Sad, Belgrade, and Pancevo a few months before lacked the capacity to drop food to hundreds of thousands of people facing starvation in the mountains to which they had been driven by the TNI forces armed and trained by the United States, and its no less cynical allies. The Administration also took no meaningful action to rescue the several hundred thousand captives held by paramilitaries in West Timor. Nor was there any notable call for such action, in particular, on the part of those who had been praising themselves for months for their high moral qualities, unrivalled in history.

As the Indonesian occupying army withdrew after Washington had given the word, an Australian-led UN peacekeeping force (INTERFET, International Force in East Timor) entered the territory on September 20 1999 and quickly took control, though not before further atrocities were carried out by the retreating forces, among them the murder of South-east Asia correspondent Sander Thoenes on September 21.[6] It may be recalled that the Indonesian invasion began in October 1975 with the murder of five Western journalists, with another killed when Indonesia invaded outright two months later.

Japan, long a fervent supporter of Indonesia, offered $100 million for INTERFET and Portugal $5 million. Washington provided no funds; the Clinton Administration asked the UN "to reduce the size" of its small peacekeeping force. That is perhaps not surprising, in the light of Washington's failure "to pay any of the $37.9 million assessed for the start-up costs of the United Nations civilian operation in Kosovo, which Washington supported in the Security Council." Seven months after INTERFET entered, the US had paid $8 million of the niggardly $13 million it had pledged in reconstruction aid, one-fifth of the total that had been delivered.[7]

By the end of 1999, 100,000–150,000 or more people remained in Indonesian West Timor as "virtual prisoners," Amnesty International reported, "trapped in makeshift camps and living in a state of constant fear under the rule of the militia groups that destroyed East Timor, . . . often intimidated, harassed, extorted and in some cases sexually assaulted and killed." This is "the only place in the world where UNHCR workers are heavily escorted by police and army troops when they go into camps," the agency reported, adding that "[t]he moment an East Timorese expresses a desire to leave the camps and go home, their life is in danger." Perhaps 500 had died "due to inadequate sanitation and medical care," officials said, mostly children, victims of diarrhoea and dysentery. "Every day, many of the people are dying from malaria, respiratory infections and acute gastro-intestinal diseases," says Arthur Howshen, a volunteer doctor. "There is also a lack of food, shortages of rice are common, and there are also a lot of children suffering from vitamin A deficiency." With the onset of the rainy season in late 1999, conditions deteriorated further. Touring camps on both sides of the border, US Assistant Secretary of State Harold Koh reported that the refugees are "starving and terrorized," and that disappearances "without explanation" are a daily occurrence. Amnesty International estimated over 100,000 refugees by late December. West Timorese officials reported 150,000. At the end of January, the Australian press reported from West Timor that over 150,000 still remained.[8]

To bring these crimes to an end has easily been within Washington's power, as before.

By January 2000, an Australian academic specialist writes,

no one really knows how many people were killed in the pre- and post-ballot period. Bodies, often in mass graves, were still being discovered, many more were believed to have been dumped in the shark-infested ocean and a disturbingly high number of people, as many as 80,000, had still not been accounted for. Many were scattered, certainly, but their shadow left a chilling sensation in anyone who stopped for a moment to consider the implications of such unaccountability[9]

– which extends far beyond Indonesia, primarily to Washington and London, though not only there.

Meanwhile, in the ravaged country,

> The frail, the old, and the children of East Timor are dying every day of preventable ailments such as gastroenteritis, which cause vomiting and diarrhoea. Besides clean water, meat or protein of any kind, cooking fuel, modern sanitation and shelter are impossible luxuries for most Timorese, even in the capital Dili. The retreating Indonesian army polluted the wells with bodies and chemicals, destroyed the water supply and phone systems, then stole everything else.[10]

In the case of Kosovo, Slobodan Milosevic and other Serbian leaders were indicted by the War Crimes Tribunal in May 1999, at the height of the NATO bombing campaign. The indictment was expedited at the initiative of Washington and London, which also provided unprecedented access to intelligence information. In East Timor, investigations were discussed at leisure, with numerous delays and deference to Jakarta's wishes and sensibilities. "It's an absolute joke, a complete whitewash," a spokeswoman for Amnesty International informed the British press: it will "cause East Timorese even more trauma than they have suffered already"; a leading Indonesian role "would be really insulting at this stage." Few seriously expect that the US or UK will release vital intelligence information, and the Indonesian generals are reported to feel confident that their old friends will not let them down – if only because the chain of responsibility might be hard to snap at just the right point. By mid-January 2000, UN officials said that a tribunal was unlikely. US Ambassador Richard Holbrooke and others "are pinning their hopes on an internal tribunal held by Indonesia, whose military controlled East Timor from 1975 until August and is blamed by human-rights groups for the atrocities." It was claimed that China and Russia are blocking a tribunal, an obstacle that the West cannot think of any way to overcome, unlike the case of Serbia.[11]

On January 31 2000, the UN International Commission of Inquiry on East Timor issued a report calling for an international human rights tribunal under UN auspices to address the matter of accountability. Its mandate should be "to try and sentence those accused by the independent investigation body of serious violations of fundamental human rights and international humanitarian law which took place in East Timor since January 1999." "It is fundamental for the future social and political stability of East Timor," the Commission concluded, "that the truth be established and those responsible for the crimes committed be brought to justice. Every effort has to be made to provide adequate reparation to the victims for only then can true reconciliation take place." Among those calling for an international tribunal, along with Amnesty International and the UN Mission, was Bishop Belo, who assigns direct responsibility for the massacres from early 1999 to army chief General Wiranto in Jakarta.[12]

On the same day, an Indonesian government Commission of Inquiry issued a "damning report" condemning "the Indonesian military and its militia surrogates" for atrocities "following the territory's August 30 vote for independence," including former

General Wiranto.[13] Indonesian President Abdurrahman Wahid, then at the Davos conference in Switzerland, called upon Wiranto to resign his cabinet post, and promised to pardon him if he is convicted. UN High Commissioner for Human Rights Mary Robinson expressed her "hope that efforts to hold those responsible for the atrocities in East Timor accountable will go on so that there is no impunity." But that is "not very likely," correspondent Dan Murphy observed: 'Support within the UN for a war-crimes tribunal is low." Crucially, support amongst the great powers is not merely "low" but negative. The general attitude is expressed by the editors of the *Washington Post*: "But before a Bosnia-style tribunal is created, Indonesia should be given a chance to judge its own" – and to pardon the most prominent of them if convicted, as the President announced at once.[14]

Australian UN correspondent Mark Riley reported from New York that the UN "is set to ignore the strong advice of its own human rights body for a war crimes tribunal in East Timor, instead deferring debate on the issue until Indonesia's probe into the killings is completed. The decision is a political victory for the Jakarta [government], which has argued that it should be left alone to investigate allegations of atrocities on what it considers was its sovereign territory." UN Secretary-General Kofi Annan "does not endorse the [international] tribunal in his accompanying letter to the report," Riley added: "the absence of a clear recommendation from Mr Annan meant that no decision was likely to be reached on a tribunal," UN officials said. The "suggestion of dual representation [jointly with Indonesia] is a significant departure from the UN tribunal models established in Rwanda and Bosnia," Riley comments, "aimed at avoiding allegations of bias in the prosecutions." Allegations of bias are a matter of concern when the perpetrators of crimes are acting with the support and complicity of the US, Britain, and their allies, so that inquiry must be controlled. But the question is academic, in the absence of an international tribunal.

Sonia Picado, head of the UN Inquiry Commission, was not optimistic, Riley reported further, recognizing "that there is little prospect of the UN Security Council supporting an international war crimes tribunal." "The East Timorese deserve compensation – moral and material compensation – because their families and their country have been devastated," Picado said, and "the UN has to give that to them": "it cannot be provided through an Indonesian tribunal." Picado "had no faith in the ability of a planned Indonesian tribunal to deliver justice to the East Timorese people." "It is just not feasible for [the Indonesians] to create a tribunal out of the blue and bring their own generals to justice," she said. Furthermore, no meaningful tribunal can be held in Jakarta because "East Timorese people remained scared of the Indonesian authorities and most were reluctant to travel to Jakarta to give evidence to a government tribunal. How can they expect the military courts in Indonesia to bring justice to the people of East Timor?" But "East Timor deserves not to be forgotten," and with an international tribunal unlikely, she recommended a South African-style Truth and Reconciliation Commission with commissioners from East Timor, Indonesia and UN-appointed members, with powers to indict or pardon, meeting outside Indonesia.[15]

Australian Asia correspondent Lindsay Murdoch commented that "grave doubts exist that the guilty will be brought to justice. Indonesia's legal system is riddled with corruption and has a poor record when dealing with human rights abuses." Indonesian Attorney-General Marzuki Darusman is "a respected human rights advocate," but "the task he faces in bringing some of the country's most powerful people to justice appears daunting, if not impossible," as illustrated by President Wahid's apparently having "buckled to pressure from General Wiranto" by declaring that he would be pardoned if found guilty: "Any such pardon would be outrageous," Murdoch wrote. Not by the criteria of Washington and London, it seems.[16]

"You cannot have one-sided justice in human rights cases," Picado said. It is fairly safe, however, to predict that one-sided justice is the most that can be anticipated, and even that is a dubious prospect. Furthermore, it is hardly likely that the guilty parties, particularly the US and Britain, will consider providing the "moral and material compensation" they owe to the victims, and there is no call for such reparations, just as there was no call for them to offer help to starving refugees driven from their homes by troops they armed and trained, or even to provide more than trivial sums for the peacekeeping force that finally put an end to the twenty-four years of horror they had imposed on the suffering people of East Timor. The responsibilities of the powerful and privileged do not extend that far in the "new era of enlightenment" grandly proclaimed by the new generation of leaders and their acolytes.

In the United States, the UN report, calling for an international tribunal into crimes committed from January 1999, received only passing mention, and the crucial issues, scant attention. There was, however, substantial coverage of (and support for) the Indonesian government tribunal, generally interpreted as focusing on the post-referendum period.[17] Similarly, virtually all discussion keeps to the picture that "the violence in East Timor was prompted by" the August 30 referendum, which set off "the rampage last year in East Timor after the province voted for independence."[18]

The restriction to that period is important for the international collaborators in the terrorist operations of the preceding months, which were murderous and destructive. Under the post-referendum restriction, one might argue without utter absurdity that there was little time for the Western powers to respond; not so if the preceding months were granted an honest exposure, not to speak of the preceding years. The Jakarta option has other advantages: East Timorese are unlikely to testify, pardon has already been announced for the chief military commander, the pressures to evade unpleasant facts will be strong, and the great powers are immune from inspection. But even in an international tribunal the possibility that Western leaders would be held accountable for their crimes is so slight as hardly to merit comment, as the International Tribunal for Kosovo demonstrated, to no one's surprise. Only by attaining a remarkable level of "intentional ignorance" can one fail to perceive that the international judicial process, like other aspects of international affairs, is subject to the rule of force, which overrules considerations of justice, human rights or accountability.

In East Timor, the peacekeeping forces and the UN mission

"have neither the means nor the authority to track down those responsible" for crimes, and little evidence is being unearthed: "in contrast to Kosovo, where human-rights investigators began work as NATO forces took control on the ground, the UN in East Timor has no such capability."[19] "Meanwhile, in East Timor, the evidence of crimes against humanity – and so the chance of successful prosecutions – is literally rotting away because of inadequate resources." UN civilian police are finding many bodies and mass graves, but have no resources to investigate them. "The need for forensic experts is very, very urgent," said David Wimhurst, spokesman for UNAMET. "Neither INTERFET nor UNAMET is able to do this properly at the moment. It is crucial that investigative teams come into Dili as soon as possible." He continued, "When NATO went into Kosovo, teams of police, forensic scientists and lawyers from the International War Crimes Tribunal in The Hague were at work within days, sealing off and cataloguing mass grave sites. In East Timor, a few harassed policemen have the task of exhuming the bodies and collecting what evidence they can."[20]

The delays ensured that little would be found, even if forensic experts had ultimately been provided at any significant level. Much of the evidence was destroyed by the TNI, bodies were buried by local people, and more would soon be washed away or eaten by animals, Australian doctor Andrew McNaughtan told the press in November, giving details informed by his experience of working in East Timor for seven years. Isabel Ferreira, who co-ordinates the East Timor Human Rights Commission in Dili, added that "when the rainy season begins, all the bodies will be washed away into the rivers and there will be no evidence left to investigate." Kosovo was swarming with police and medical forensic teams from the US and other countries in the hope of discovering large-scale atrocities. In East Timor, in contrast, it is important that the record remain hidden. INTERFET had ten investigators, no morgue, and no forensic capabilities. Australian forensic pathologists confirmed in November that tropical heat and the onset of the rainy season would soon eliminate most evidence. UN Administrator Sergio Vieira de Mello pleaded again for forensic experts and facilities at the end of November, in vain. A month later it was announced that "international forensic experts will arrive in January to help in investigations of mass graves" and to compile information on crimes – four months after the arrival of INTERFET, long after tropical rains and other factors had significantly reduced the likelihood of revealing the truth about what had taken place.[21]

The distinction between the two most prominent atrocities of 1999 is clear. In Kosovo, there was a desperate need for tribunal indictment. Furthermore, "proving the scale of the crimes is also important to NATO politically, to show why 78 days of airstrikes against Serbian forces and infrastructure were necessary," by the intriguing logic, conventional in Western doctrine, that Serbian crimes provide retrospective justification for the NATO bombing of which they were the anticipated consequence.[22] Putting logic aside, at least the immediate agent of the crimes in Kosovo is an official enemy, while in East Timor, the agents of the crimes were armed, trained, funded and supported by the US and its allies from the beginning through the terrible denouement. It is therefore advisable to know as little as possible about the crimes, so as to mitigate the threat that rational conclusions will be drawn.

The preferred conclusions have passed through several phases. During the worst years, in the late 1970s, when aggression and violence carried out with US arms and diplomatic support reached horrendous levels, the reaction was silence, broken by occasional transmission of lies of the State Department and Indonesian generals. After they had given the "green light" and the shocking facts began to emerge, the picture shifted to "the shaming of Indonesia," in "a typical South-east Asian war – in which cruelty knew few bounds and both sides pushed and pulled a largely unpolitical people in order to deny them to the 'enemy'" (editors, South-east Asia correspondent Henry Kamm, *New York Times*). There was no "shaming of the US," and cruelty is unknown in the wars of Europe and its outposts. Some commentators, like Asia specialist Stanley Karnow and foreign correspondent Richard Valeriani, felt that even this much attention, omitting entirely the US role, was superfluous and indeed irritating. After all, nothing significant is at stake; only the fact that "Washington has armed and trained an Indonesian military responsible for the most intensive mass killings since World War II," a leading Australian Asia journal observes. Later, as the enormity of what had happened began to reach the public, it was conceded that the US "averted its eyes from East Timor" and "could have done far more than it did to distance itself from the carnage" (James Fallows) – that is, the carnage that it implemented with enthusiasm and dedication. As in the case of the Kurds, the US "tolerated" the atrocities in East Timor and "failed to protect" the victims.[23]

The current version is that the "Pentagon's Investment in Indonesia Lacks Payoff" and "America's efforts to gain influence by training officers are for naught, as the violence in East Timor demonstrates." "For years, the Pentagon has spent millions on programs that aim not only to train fast-rising officers in foreign armies – including Indonesia's – but to plant in them the seeds of American values and influence."[24] For thirty-five years in the case of Indonesia. There and elsewhere, the values implanted have led to brutal state terror with remarkable consistency, and in close conformity to the doctrines that are taught and that are followed by the tutors themselves when the need arises. Somehow, none of this raises questions about what these "American values" might be. Nor does it seem relevant that high-level planners have been most impressed by the "payoff" from the military "investment in Indonesia," particularly after its most stunning achievement in 1965.[25]

While TNI forces and their paramilitaries ("militias") were burning down the capital city of Dili in September 1999, murdering and rampaging with renewed intensity, the Pentagon announced that "A US–Indonesian training exercise focused on humanitarian and disaster relief activities concluded August 25," five days before the referendum.[26] The lessons were quickly applied in the familiar way, as all but the voluntarily blind must recognize after many years of the same tales, the same outcomes.

One gruesome illustration was the coup that brought General Suharto to power in 1965. Army-led massacres slaughtered hundreds of thousands in a few months, mostly landless peasants, destroying the mass-based political party of the left, the PKI, in "one of the worst mass murders of the twentieth century," the CIA concluded, ranking with "the Soviet purges of the 1930s, the Nazi mass murders during the Second World War, and the Maoist bloodbath of the early 1950s."[27]

The Rwanda-style slaughter in Indonesia elicited unrestrained euphoria in the West and fulsome praise for the Indonesian "moderates," Suharto and his military accomplices, who had eliminated the rot, and for the US government, which had helped implement the great events while wisely keeping its role under wraps so as not to embarrass the moderates. The highly respected *New York Times* commentator James Reston welcomed "the savage transformation of Indonesia" under the heading "A Gleam of Light in Asia," reporting – presumably on the basis of high-level leaks – that "Washington is being careful not to claim any credit for this change," though "it is doubtful if the coup would ever have been attempted without the American show of strength in Vietnam or been sustained without the clandestine aid it has received indirectly from here." Secretary of Defense Robert McNamara informed Congress that US military aid and training had "paid dividends" – including half a million or more corpses; "enormous dividends," a congressional report concluded. McNamara informed President Johnson that US military assistance "encouraged [the army] to move against the PKI when the opportunity was presented." Contacts with Indonesian military officers, including university programs, were "very significant factors in determining the favorable orientation of the new Indonesian political elite" (the army). The US had "trained 4000 Indonesian army officers – half the total officer corps, including one-third of the general staff," two Australian analysts observe.[28]

Not surprisingly, the reaction to the slaughter has been excised from history, though not entirely. Years later McGeorge Bundy, National Security Adviser under Presidents Kennedy and Johnson, finally came to realize that "our effort" in Vietnam might well have been ended after October 1965, when "a new anti-Communist government took power in Indonesia and destroyed the Communist Party." With Indonesia now protected from infection, it may have been "excessive" to continue to demolish Indochina at inordinate cost to ourselves, he explained, recognizing clearly the real motives for the US attack against South Vietnam, then all of Indochina, and also the nature of the partial US victory in that war. In his memoirs, Kennedy–Johnson Secretary of Defense Robert McNamara observes with admiration that Indonesia "reversed course" after the killing of "300,000 or more PKI members . . . and now lay in the hands of independent nationalists led by Suharto." He describes his frustration over the irrational refusal of the Vietnamese enemy to accept his offer of a negotiated settlement on the model of the "independent nationalism" of Suharto's Indonesia, in which they would lay down their arms in an "independent, non-Communist South Vietnam," which might then treat the South Vietnamese resistance – the only "truly mass-based political party in South Vietnam," according to the assessment of US government Indochina expert Douglas Pike – with the kindness lavished on the only mass-based political party in Indonesia by its "moderate independent nationalists."[29]

The US is a global power, and policies tend to be consistent worldwide. At the same time, the same planners were helping to institute murderous military terror states elsewhere, on the principle, explained by McNamara to McGeorge Bundy, that it is the task of the military to remove civilian leaders from office "whenever, in the judgment of the military, the conduct of these leaders is injurious to the welfare of the nation," a necessity in "the Latin American cultural environment," and likely to be carried out properly now that the judgment of the military is based upon "the understanding of, and orientation toward, US objectives" as a result of the military aid and training provided by the Kennedy Administration.[30]

So matters continued in Indonesia for three decades of military aid, training, and friendly interaction with the great mass murderer and torturer who was "at heart benign," the London *Economist* explained, and unfairly condemned by "propagandists for the guerrillas" in East Timor and West Papua (Irian Jaya) who "talk of the army's savagery and use of torture." The unnamed propagandists were the major international human rights groups, the Timorese Church, and others who failed to see the merits of "our kind of guy," as the Clinton Administration admiringly described Suharto when he was welcomed to Washington in October 1995. His son-in-law General Prabowo, "the leader of Indonesia's paramilitary death squads, who has authorised mass killings and rapes" and was finally sent to Jordan as an embarrassment after the fall of Suharto, was "an 'enlightened' military leader who deserved to have his demands treated promptly and with courtesy by British politicians," according to British Defence Minister George Robertson, "liberator of oppressed muslims of Kosovo."[31]

Direct US support for Indonesian occupation forces in East

Timor became more difficult after they massacred several hundred people in Dili in 1991, an atrocity that could not be suppressed or denied because it was secretly filmed by photojournalist Max Stahl and played on TV in the UK and US, and because two US journalists, Alan Nairn and Amy Goodman, who were severely beaten, were able to give eyewitness reports. In reaction, Congress banned small arms sales and cut off funds for military training, compelling the Clinton Administration to resort to some intricate maneuvers to evade the legislative restrictions, as it was doing in Turkey at the same time. The State Department commemorated the anniversary of the Indonesian invasion by determining that "Congress's action did not ban Indonesia's purchase of training with its own funds," so the training can proceed despite the ban, with Washington perhaps paying from some other pocket. The announcement received scant notice and no comment in the press, but it did lead Congress to express its "outrage," reiterating that "it was and is the intent of Congress to prohibit US military training for Indonesia" (House Appropriations Committee): "We don't want employees of the US Government training Indonesians," a staff member reiterated forcefully, but without effect.[32]

Government-approved weapons sales come to over $1 billion since the 1975 invasion, including $150 million during the Clinton years; government-licensed sales of armaments increased from $3.3 million to $16.3 million from fiscal 1997 to 1998.[33] As atrocities peaked in 1977–78, the UK, France, and others joined the US in providing arms for the killers as well as diplomatic protection.

Britain's Hawk jets proved to be particularly effective for

killing and terrorizing civilians. The current Labour government continued to deliver Hawk jets to Indonesia, using public funds, as late as September 23 1999, two weeks after the European Union had imposed an embargo; three days after INTERFET had landed, well after it had been revealed that these aircraft had been deployed over East Timor once again, this time as part of the pre-referendum intimidation operation; and two weeks after the Indonesian Air Force had deployed British Hawks at the Kupang Airbase in West Timor "to anticipate any intrusion of foreign aircraft into the eastern part of Indonesian territory, especially East Timor." Under New Labour, Britain became the leading supplier of arms to Indonesia, despite the strong protests of Amnesty International, Indonesian dissidents, and Timorese victims. Foreign Secretary Robin Cook, the author of the new "ethical foreign policy," explained that "the government is committed to the maintenance of a strong defence industry, which is a strategic part of our industrial base," as in the US and elsewhere. For the same reasons, Prime Minister Tony Blair later gave "the go-ahead for the sale of spare parts to Zimbabwe for British Hawk fighter jets being used in an African civil war that has cost tens of thousands of lives."[34]

Perhaps, nonetheless, the "new generation draws the line" a shade to the ethical side of their Tory predecessors, whose position, as expressed by Thatcherite defense procurement minister Alan Clark, was that: "My responsibility is to my own people. I don't really fill my mind much with what one set of foreigners is doing to another."[35] However that may be, these are altogether unsurprising illustrations of the new humanism, a grand new era in world affairs led by the United States, now "at the height of its glory,"[36] and its British partner.

In 1997 the Pentagon was still training Indonesian military forces. The programs continued into 1998 under the code name Iron Balance, "hidden from legislators and the public" because they were in violation of the clear intent of congressional restrictions. "Principal among the units that continued to be trained was the Kopassus – an elite force with a bloody history – which was more rigorously trained by the US than any other Indonesian unit," according to Pentagon documents. Training focused on "military expertise that could only be used internally against civilians, such as urban guerrilla warfare, surveillance, counter-intelligence, sniper marksmanship and 'psychological operations'." Among commanders trained were those implicated in the renewed outburst of violence in 1999, as well as earlier massacres, including Krasas in 1983 and Dili in 1991. "Loyal" Timorese also received US training. Britain was carrying out similar programs.[37]

From 1997 and with particular intensity through 1998, "East Timor was being used as a training ground for the army's elite troops," which were "directly supervising teams of paramilitary" in a "build-up [that] was obvious" on the ground. TNI military personnel documents leaked in August 1998 provided details on the paramilitary units controlled by Kopassus. Even before that, Australian aid workers had been providing information to the Australian government on "the worrying build-up of [TNI-] supported militia."[38]

In November 1998, Kopassus forces arrived in a port town in East Timor, entering in disguise along with the first of 5,000 new TNI forces recruited from West Timor and elsewhere in Indonesia. These became the core elements of the paramilitaries that initiated massive violence in operation "Clean Sweep" from February 1999, with "the aim, quite simply, . . . to destroy a nation." As senior military adviser, the military command sent General Makarim, a US-trained intelligence specialist with experience in East Timor and "a reputation for callous violence"; he was also assigned the role of liaison with the UN observer mission. In the last few months of 1998, "hundreds were killed, hundreds more disappeared, and thousands were uprooted from their homes" with "violent oppression," Australian aid director Lansell Taudevin reports. Atrocities mounted through January, increasingly assigned to the Kopassus-run paramilitaries in the classic fashion, familiar from recent practice in Turkey, Colombia, Kosovo, and elsewhere. The plans and their implementation were, surely, known to Western intelligence.[39]

There has been no serious doubt that from the beginning of 1999, the atrocities attributed to militias were organized, directed, and sometimes carried out by elite units of Kopassus, the "crack special forces unit" that had "been training regularly with US and Australian forces until their behaviour became too much of an embarrassment for their foreign friends," veteran Asia correspondent David Jenkins reports; though not their friends in Washington, it appears. These forces are "legendary for their cruelty," Benedict Anderson observes: in East Timor they "became the pioneer and exemplar for every kind of atrocity," including systematic rapes, tortures and executions, and organization of hooded gangsters. They adopted the tactics of the US Phoenix program in South Vietnam that killed tens of thousands of peasants and much of the indigenous South Vietnamese leadership, Jenkins writes, as well as "the tactics employed by the Contras" in Nicaragua, following lessons taught by their CIA mentors. The state terrorists were "not simply going after the most radical pro-independence people but going after the moderates, the people who have influence in their community." "It's Phoenix," a well-placed source in Jakarta reported: the aim is "to terrorise everyone" – the NGOs, the Red Cross, the UN, the journalists.[40]

There is also no serious doubt that Australian intelligence, and US and British intelligence as well, knew all of this, and had known the full details for twenty-five years, from information provided by the Defence Signals Directorate base in northern Australia and many other sources. It is hard to imagine that the civilian authorities were unaware of what they were supporting.

By April–May 1999 the Australian government "finally and formally acknowledged that the military was behind paramilitary atrocities."[41] Des Ball, the leading Australian academic specialist on intelligence issues, reports that from April 1999 intelligence was coming from a wide range of sources "which provided very detailed evidence firstly of particular working relationships between units of the Indonesian Army and particular militia elements and militia leaders, but also provided even more direct and explicit evidence of Wiranto's direct involvement in the arming and supporting of the militia." On April 20, Australian intelligence reported that "Indonesian military officers are actively supporting pro-Indonesian militants in East Timor," implicating Wiranto. At the same time Indonesian army and militia commanders warned that if the population persisted in seeking independence, they would "liquidate all the CNRT [pro-independence organization], all the pro-independence people, parents, sons, daughters and grandchildren," following the orders of Indonesian regional military commander Adam Damiri; the information was transmitted quickly to Australian intelligence. When the UN observer mission UNAMET arrived a month later, "they began putting together a virtual library of evidence establishing the conspiracy between the military and the militias."[42]

TNI forces responsible for the terror and destruction from February have been described as "rogue elements" in the West. There is, however, ample reason to accept the judgment of Bishop Belo and others that direct responsibility traces directly back to TNI commander Wiranto in Jakarta,[43] not only in the post-referendum period to which attention is largely restricted.

From February through July, 3–5,000 East Timorese were killed according to highly credible Church sources.[44] The terror was widespread and sadistic, intended as a warning to the Timorese of the fate awaiting them if they were foolhardy enough to disregard army orders, and presumably to others in Indonesia itself who might be tempted to adopt a similar stance.

The events were reported widely in Australia, to some extent in England. In Australia there was extensive protest along with calls for action to end the atrocities. Though information was much more sparse,[45] there was mounting protest in the US as well. On June 22, the Senate unanimously supported an amendment to a State Department authorization bill asking the

Clinton Administration to "intensify their efforts to prevail upon the Indonesian government and military" to crack down on the militias, reiterated on June 30 by a vote of 98–0. In a July 8 press briefing, in response to a query about the Senate vote, State Department spokesperson James Foley repeated the official stand that "the Indonesian military has a responsibility to bring those militias under control" – namely, the militias it was organizing, arming, and directing.[46] Once again, database searches found no report of any of this in the US.

Well before the referendum, the commander of the Indonesian military in Dili, Colonel Tono Suratman, had warned of what was to come: "I would like to convey the following," he said: "if the pro-independents do win . . . all will be destroyed . . . It will be worse than 23 years ago." On July 24, Suratman met with a police commander and militia leaders at the Dili military headquarters, where they took "the major decisions . . . in the recognition that the pro-integration side was unlikely to win the vote," according to an August 6 report by Australian intelligence officer Wayne Sievers. Sievers is now facing charges for having informed the Parliament's Committee on Foreign Affairs, Defence and Trade of the secret reports he had sent to the UN from his arrival in June, predicting the post-referendum violence and identifying militia leaders as Indonesian intelligence officers, all of this available to the Australian government through its UN Embassy. A TNI document of early May, when the UN–Indonesia–Portugal agreement on the referendum was reached, ordered that "[m]assacres should be carried out from village to village after the announcement of the ballot if the pro-independence supporters win."

The independence movement "should be eliminated from its leadership down to its roots."[47]

Documents discovered in Dili in October 1999, "and analysed in Jakarta by Indonesian investigators and Western diplomatic sources, provide evidence . . . that, for months before the referendum on East Timor's independence in August, it was being systematically undermined by Indonesia's top generals," including plans for "the forcible deportation of hundreds of thousands of East Timorese." A Western diplomat who reviewed the documents describes them as "the missing link," showing "a clear chain of command from close to the very top," also expressing his surprise at the "sheer quantity" of the weapons provided to local militia and pro-Jakarta figures. As the May 5 referendum agreement was signed, a letter from General Subagyo to Colonel Suratman, copied to senior military figures, ordered preparations for "a security plan to prevent civil war that includes preventive action (create conditions), policing measures, repressive/coercive measures and a plan to move to the rear/evacuate if the second option [independence] is chosen." A July document drafted by an officer of a Dili-based regional command, Colonel Soedjarwo, outlines a battle plan directed against what it calls the "Enemy Forces": "not only the guerrillas of the resistance movement, Falintil, but civilians, including unarmed student groups and political organisations." In August, the Dili police department produced "a meticulous plan to evacuate hundreds of thousands of Timorese after the referendum," with extensive detail. The plans were soon implemented, and it would be most surprising if they were not known at least in a general way to Western intelligence.[48]

Citing diplomatic, church and militia sources, the Australian press had reported in July 1999 that "hundreds of modern assault rifles, grenades and mortars are being stockpiled, ready for use if the autonomy option is rejected at the ballot box." It warned that the army-run militias might be planning a violent takeover of much of the territory if, despite the terror, the popular will would be expressed. Leaked official cables reveal the "Australian government's harsh assessment of the Pentagon's 'overly generous' interpretation of Indonesian army (TNI) involvement with the militias."[49] The Indonesian generals had every reason to interpret the evasive and ambiguous reactions of their traditional friends and backers as a "green light" to carry out their work.

One may compare the reaction in the enlightened West to the plans of Indonesia and of Serbia for large-scale ethnic cleansing and destruction. In the former case, explicit, known, disregarded; in the latter, "discovered" two weeks after the bombing began and probably fabricated (Operation Horseshoe), though doubtless such plans existed. In the former case, the responsibility of the "new generation"; in the latter, attributed to an official enemy as a justification for bombing.

The pace of terror escalated in April 1999, including major massacres, as at Liquica, when some sixty people – or perhaps far more – were murdered in a church where they had taken shelter. Western investigators on the scene now believe that 200 or more were murdered. An American police officer comments that "officially we must stay with the number of bodies that we have actually lifted, but the total number of people killed in this district is much, much higher than that, perhaps even astro-nomical." The full story will never be known, in this and other cases, because of the unwillingness of the West to permit serious investigation.[50]

A few days after the Liquica massacre, Admiral Dennis Blair, US Pacific Commander, met with TNI commander General Wiranto, assuring him of US support and assistance and pro-posing a new US training mission, one of several such contacts.[51]

In the face of this record, only briefly sampled, and dupli-cated repeatedly elsewhere, Washington lauds "the value of the years of training given to Indonesia's future military leaders in the United States and the millions of dollars in military aid for Indonesia," urging more of the same for Indonesia and throughout the world, though commentators acknowledge that the huge training programs have somehow failed "to plant in them the seeds of American values and influence."[52]

The reasons for the disgraceful record have sometimes been honestly recognized. During the final phase of atrocities, a senior diplomat in Jakarta formulated "the dilemma" faced by the great powers succinctly: "Indonesia matters and East Timor doesn't."[53] It is therefore understandable that Washington should keep to ineffectual gestures of disapproval while insisting that internal security in East Timor "is the responsibility of the government of Indonesia, and we don't want to take that responsibility away from them" – the official stance throughout, repeated a few days before the August referendum in full knowl-edge of how that responsibility had been carried out. The same position was officially reiterated well after the referendum, while the most dire predictions were being fulfilled.[54] As noted, the same doctrine underlies the insistence that further inquiry into the crimes must be the responsibility of Indonesia, not an international tribunal.

The reasoning of the senior diplomat was spelled out more fully by two Asia specialists of the *New York Times*: the Clinton Administration "has made the calculation that the United States must put its relationship with Indonesia, a mineral-rich nation of more than 200 million people, ahead of its concern over the political fate of East Timor, a tiny impoverished territory of 800,000 people that is seeking independence." The second national journal quoted Douglas Paal, President of the Asia Pacific Policy Center: "Timor is a speed bump on the road to dealing with Jakarta, and we've got to get over it safely. Indonesia is such a big place and so central to the stability of the region."[55]

The term "stability" has long served as a code word, referring to what former Secretary of Defence Robert McNamara called a "favorable orientation of the political elite" – favorable not to their populations but to foreign investors and global managers.[56]

In the rhetoric of official Washington through 1999, "We don't have a dog running in the East Timor race." Accordingly, what happens there is not our concern. But after intensive Australian pressure, the calculations shifted: "we have a very big dog running down there called Australia and we have to support it," a senior government official concluded.[57] The survivors of US-backed crimes in a "tiny impoverished territory" are not even a small dog.

Commenting on Washington's stance, the veteran Australian diplomat Richard Butler observed that "it has been made very clear to me by senior American analysts that the facts of the [US–Australia] alliance essentially are that: the US will respond proportionally, defined largely in terms of its own interests and threat assessment . . ." The remarks were not offered in criticism of Washington. Rather, of his fellow Australians, who do not comprehend the facts of life: others are to shoulder the burdens and face the costs, unless some power interest is served, in the new era of enlightenment and high principle.[58]

Serious commentators had recognized these realities long before. Twenty years earlier, correspondent Daniel Southerland reported that "in deferring to Indonesia on [the East Timor] issue, the Carter Administration, like the Ford Administration before it, appears to have placed big-power concerns ahead of human rights." Southerland referred particularly to the crucial role of current UN Ambassador Richard Holbrooke, who had direct responsibility for implementing Carter's policy of support for Indonesian aggression and slaughter, and was so little concerned by the consequences – by then, some 200,000 killed – that he could find no time to testify before Congress about East Timor, Southerland reports, though "he did have the time, however, to play host at a black-tie dinner later the same day."[59]

History is reconstructed, however, to convey a different image. With the past obliterated, Holbrooke is depicted as the hero of "the swiftest response [to atrocities] in the history of UN peacekeeping," and "the first time in the post-Rwanda, post-Srebrenica era that the Security Council met an emergency head-on" – namely, after the country had been destroyed and its population expelled or killed, in accord with plans that were surely known to Washington well in advance. Now UN Ambassador, Holbrooke

> described the operation as the textbook realization of Churchill and Roosevelt's dream when they laid out the principles of the UN. "It took only twenty years, a staggering number of wasted lives, and pillaging and rampaging by the Indonesian military," Holbrooke grimly added.

His role in establishing these conditions is unmentioned, as is the US role throughout, apart from a reference to Clinton's "temporizing for several days" before threatening to veto loans to Indonesia.[60]

The guiding principles were well understood from the outset by those responsible for guaranteeing the success of Indonesia's 1975 invasion. They were articulated lucidly by UN Ambassador Daniel Patrick Moynihan, in words that should be committed to memory by anyone with a serious interest in international affairs, human rights, and the rule of law. The Security Council condemned the invasion and ordered Indonesia to withdraw, but to no avail. In his 1978 memoirs, Moynihan explains why:

> The United States wished things to turn out as they did, and worked to bring this about. The Department of State desired that the United Nations prove utterly ineffective in whatever measures it undertook. This task was given to me, and I carried it forward with no inconsiderable success.

Success was indeed considerable. Moynihan cites reports that within two months some 60,000 people had been killed, "10 per cent of the population, almost the proportion of casualties experienced by the Soviet Union during the Second World War."[61] A sign of the success, he adds, is that within a year "the subject disappeared from the press." So it did, as the invaders intensified their assault. Atrocities peaked as Moynihan was writing in 1977–78. Relying on a new flow of US military equipment, the Indonesian military carried out a devastating attack against the hundreds of thousands who had fled to the mountains, driving the survivors to Indonesian control. It was then that Church sources in East Timor sought to make public the estimates of 200,000 deaths that came to be accepted years later, after constant denial and ridicule of the "propagandists for the guerrillas." Washington's reaction to the carnage has already been described.

Media coverage of East Timor had been fairly high prior to the Indonesian invasion, in the context of concerns over the collapse of Portuguese fascism and its imperial system. Coverage declined as the US-supported aggression and slaughter took its toll; in the national press it fell to zero as atrocities reached near-genocidal levels in 1978. Journals were similar.[62] Such coverage as there was during the worst atrocities kept largely to State Department fabrications and assurances from Indonesian generals that the population was fleeing to their protection. By 1980, however, the story was beginning to break through, though the US responsibility remains well concealed to the present. By then, it was also becoming clear that the atrocities were comparable to Cambodia in the same years, though in this case they were major war crimes in addition to crimes against humanity, committed in the course of outright aggression supported by the great powers.

The first reports to break the silence caused considerable annoyance. Commenting in a journalism review, Stanley Karnow said he could not bring himself to read a story on East Timor that had just appeared: 'it didn't have anything to do with me," he said. His colleague Richard Valeriani agreed, because "I don't care about Timor." Reviewing a book that gave the first extensive account of what had happened, and the unwillingness to report it, former *New York Times* Indochina correspondent A. J. Langguth dismissed the topic on the grounds that, "If the world press were to converge suddenly on Timor, it would not improve the lot of a single Cambodian." The point was elegantly phrased by the editor of the Paris left-wing journal *Nouvel Observateur.* "History has its principal currents, and the principal current passes through Cambodia, not Timor."[63]

The observations on Timor and Cambodia are surely accurate. More important, they capture lucidly the guiding criteria for humanitarian concerns: atrocities for which we bear responsibility, and which we could easily mitigate or terminate, do not "have anything to do with" us and should be of no particular concern; worse still, they are a diversion from the morally significant task of lamenting atrocities committed by official enemies that we can do little if anything about. Though when the Vietnamese did end them in this case, Washington undertook its obligation to punish the Vietnamese for this shocking crime by severe sanctions, the backing of a Chinese invasion, and support for the ousted Khmer Rouge ("Democratic Kampuchea," DK).

Some nevertheless felt uneasy that while bitterly denouncing atrocities in Cambodia, we were "looking away" from comparable ones in Timor – the standard rendition of the unacceptable truth that Washington was "looking right there," and acting decisively to escalate the atrocities. That quandary was put to rest in 1982 by the State Department, which explained that the Khmer Rouge-based DK is "unquestionably" more representative of the people of Cambodia than the resistance is of the East Timorese, so therefore it is proper to support both Pol Pot and Suharto. The contradiction vanishes, as did the grounds for its resolution, which were unreported, and remain so.[64]

For the next twenty years the grim story continued: atrocities, Western complicity, and refusal to submit. By 1998, a few rays of hope began to break through. By then Suharto had committed some real misdeeds, and was therefore no longer "our kind of guy": he had lost control of the country after the financial crisis, and was dragging his feet on implementing harsh IMF programs. Debt relief had been granted to the "Indonesian moderate" after he took power, but not to the 200 million Indonesians who are now compelled to pay the huge debts accumulated by Suharto and his cronies, amounting now to over 140 per cent of GDP, thanks to the corruption of the regime and the eagerness of the World Bank, the IMF, and Western governments and financial institutions to provide lavish funds for the ruler and his clique, and the IMF's role as "the credit community's enforcer," in the words of its current US executive director.[65]

On May 20 1998, Secretary of State Madeleine Albright called upon Suharto to resign and provide for "a democratic transition." A few hours later, Suharto transferred formal authority to his hand-picked Vice-President B. J. Habibie. The events were not, of course, simple cause and effect, but they symbolize the relations that prevail. With Suharto gone, the way was paved for the first democratic election in forty years – that is, the first election since the parliamentary system was undermined in the course of the US clandestine operations of 1958 that aimed to dismantle Indonesia by separating the resource-rich outer islands, undertaken because of Washington's concern that the government of Indonesia was too independent and too democratic, even going so far as to permit a popular party of the left to function.[66]

There was great praise for Indonesia's first democratic election in forty years, another demonstration of our inspiring role in bringing democracy to a backward world. The commentary managed to overlook the background, which is consigned to the (ample) category of "veiled operations" – among the facts that "it 'wouldn't do' to mention," in Orwell's phrase, discussing "voluntary censorship" in free societies.

Habibie moved at once to distance himself from Suharto, surprising many observers. In June 1998, he called for a "special status" for East Timor. In August Foreign Minister Ali Alatas suggested a "wide-ranging autonomy."

On January 27 1999, Habibie made the unexpected announcement that if the East Timorese are not willing to accept Indonesia's offer of autonomy, then the government would recommend to the People's Consultative Assembly that Indonesia relinquish control of the territory it had invaded and annexed. On May 5, Indonesia and Portugal, under UN auspices, agreed that the choice should be made in a referendum scheduled at first for August 8, but delayed until August 30.

The military, however, was following a different track, already described, moving even before Habibie's January announcement to prevent a free choice by terror and intimidation.

In an astonishing display of courage, almost the entire population, braving violence and threats, made their way to the polls on August 30, many emerging from hiding to do so. Close to 80 per cent chose independence. Then followed the latest phase of TNI atrocities in an effort to reverse the outcome by slaughter and expulsion, while reducing much of the country to ashes. For the reasons already discussed, the truth of the matter will never be known, along with what preceded.

The sordid history should be viewed against the background of US-Indonesia relations in the post-war era.[67] The rich resources of the archipelago, and its critical strategic location, guaranteed it a central role in US global planning. These factors lie behind Washington's efforts forty years ago to dismantle Indonesia, then its support for the military in preparation for the anticipated coup, and unbounded enthusiasm for the regime of killers and torturers who brought about a "favorable orientation" in 1965 and for their leader, who remained "our kind of guy" until his first missteps in 1997, when he was abandoned in the usual pattern of criminals who have lost their usefulness or become disobedient: Trujillo, Somoza, Marcos, Noriega, Saddam Hussein, Mobutu, Ceausescu, and many others. As noted, the successful cleansing of Indonesia in 1965, apart from turning this rich country into a "paradise for investors," was understood to be a vindication of Washington's wars in Indochina, which were motivated in large part by concern that the "virus" of independent nationalism might "infect" Indonesia, to borrow standard rhetoric, just as concern over Indonesian independence (and later, its excessive democracy) had been motivated by fear that a "Communist" (meaning independent nationalist) Indonesia would be an "infection" that "would sweep westward" through all of South Asia, as George Kennan warned in 1948.

In this context, support for the invasion of East Timor and subsequent atrocities was presumably reflexive, though a broader analysis should attend to the fact that the collapse of the Portuguese empire had similar consequences in Africa, where South Africa rather than Indonesia was the agent of Western-backed terror. Throughout, Cold War pretexts were routinely invoked. These should be analyzed with caution; quite commonly a careful inquiry reveals that they serve as a convenient disguise for ugly motives and actions that had little to do with shifting relations among the US, Russia, and China, not only in South-east Asia but in Latin America, the Middle East, and elsewhere.

The story does not begin in 1975. East Timor had not been overlooked by the planners of the post-war world. The territory should be granted independence, Roosevelt's senior adviser Sumner Welles mused, but "it would certainly take a thousand years."[68] With an awe-inspiring display of courage and fortitude, the people of East Timor have struggled to confound that prediction, enduring monstrous disasters. Some 50,000 lost their lives protecting a small contingent of Australian commandoes fighting the Japanese; their heroism may have saved Australia from Japanese invasion. Perhaps a third of the population were victims of the first years of the 1975 Indonesian invasion, many more since.

Surely we should by now be willing to cast aside mythology and face the causes and consequences of our actions realistically, not only in East Timor. In that tortured corner of the world we now have an opportunity to remedy in some measure at least one of the most appalling crimes and tragedies of the terrible century that has finally come to a horrifying, wrenching close.

Notes

1. Report to the Security Council Mission to Jakarta and Dili, 8–12 September 1999.
2. John Roosa, "Fatal Trust in Timor," *New York Times* (henceforth *NYT*) op-ed, September 15 1999.
3. Rajiv Chandrasekaran, "US resumes training Indonesian officers," *Washington Post–Boston Globe* (henceforth *WP–BG*), February 19; Elizabeth Becker, "United States and Indonesia Quietly Resume Military Cooperation," *NYT*, May 24 2000.
4. Benedict Anderson, Statement before the Fourth Committee of the UN General Assembly, October 20 1980. For fuller quotes and context, see my *Towards a New Cold War* (New York: Pantheon, 1982). On the background, see Noam Chomsky and Edward Herman, *The Political Economy of Human Rights* (Boston: South End, 1979), vol. I.
5. Seth Mydans, "East Timor, Stuck at 'Ground Zero,' Lacks Law, Order and Much More," *NYT*, February 16 2000. On killings before the referendum, see below. Philip Shenon, "Timorese Bishop is Calling For a War Crimes Tribunal," *NYT*, September 13 1999. On

Belo and relevant history, see Arnold Kohen, *From the Place of the Dead* (New York: St. Martin's, 1999; updated 2000).

6. Cameron Barr, "A Brutal Exit: Battalion 745," *Christian Science Monitor*, March 13, 14, 16, 17, 2000.

7. Barbara Crossette, "U.N. to Begin Taking Refugees Home to East Timor This Week," *NYT*, October 5, "Annan Says U.N. Must Take Over East Timor Rule," October 6; Joe Lauria, "US asks UN for trims in force for East Timor," *Boston Globe* (henceforth *BG*), October 8 1999. Editorial, "Stumbling Efforts in East Timor," *NYT*, April 29 2000; $500 million had been pledged by international donors.

8. Amnesty International report of December 22; "Refugees in West Timor living in fear: Amnesty," AAP, Canberra, December 22 1999. "More than 150,000 East Timorese begin 5th month in West," AFP, *Age* (Australia), January 31 2000. "Up to 500 East Timorese died in West Timor camps," AP, January 13; Richard Lloyd Parry, "Forgotten: the child refugees of West Timor," *Independent* (London), January 24 2000. Koh, Slobodan Lekic, AP, "US adds choppers, specialists in E. Timor," *BG*, October 10 1999. UNHCR, see Human Rights Watch, *Forced Expulsions to West Timor and the Refugee Crisis*, December 1999.

9. Damien Kingsbury, Executive Officer of the Monash Asia Institute, "Conclusion," in Kingsbury, ed., *Guns and Ballot Boxes: East Timor's Vote for Independence* (Victoria, Australia: Monash Asia Institute, 2000).

10. Jan Mayman, Dili, "Fighting for Survival," *Far Eastern Economic Review*, February 24 2000.

11. Mark Riley, New York, "Atrocities inquiry awaits green light," *Sydney Morning Herald*, October 16; Richard Lloyd Parry, Dili, "Jakarta is Given Role in the UN's War Crimes Inquiry," *Independent*, September 27 1999. Joe Lauria, "Envoys seek inquiry by Indonesia," *BG*, January 15 2000.

12. United Nations Office of the High Commissioner for Human Rights, Report of the International Commission of Inquiry on East Timor to the Secretary-General, January; full text, February 2 2000. See also Amnesty International News Release, January 31 2000, urging the UN "to act without delay on the recommendations" of the Commission. Shenon, op. cit.

13. Keith Richburg, "Jakarta confirms E. Timor killings," *WP–BG*, February 1 2000. Also Seth Mydans, "Jakarta's Military Chiefs

Accused of Crimes," *NYT*, February 1; "Indonesian General Denies Guilt in Timor Abuses," *NYT*, February 2 2000. The Indonesian report in fact called for an inquiry reaching back to January 1999, but the US news reports cited may well prove accurate as an assessment of the prospects.

14. Dan Murphy, "E. Timor inquiry taints top brass," *Christian Science Monitor* (henceforth *CSM*) February 2; Editorial, "Justice for East Timor," *WP – International Herald Tribune*, February 2 2000.

15. Mark Riley, "UN to delay decision on crimes tribunal," *Age*, January 31; "UN official doubts Jakarta probe," February 2 2000.

16. Lindsay Murdoch, "Rights report exposes military perfidy," *Age*, February 2 2000.

17. See references cited, among many others.

18. Chandrasekran, Becker, op. cit., typical examples.

19. Cameron Barr, "Who will investigate atrocities?, "*CSM*, September 30 1999.

20. Parry, see note 11.

21. "Human rights activists decry slow UN probe in E. Timor," Kyodo News International, Dili, November 8; Sonny Inbaraj, "Rights–East Timor: Investigation into Abuses a Tricky Task," Inter Press Service, November 10; "U.N. chief in E. Timor appeals for urgent forensic help," Japan Economic Newswire, November 28; "East Timor to judge on crimes, says head of UN transition authority," AP Worldstream, AP Online, December 24 1999.

22. Scott Peterson, "This time, war-crimes trail is on a fast track," *CSM*, August 27 1999. On the indictment and other documentary sources made public in an effort to justify the bombing, and related matters, see *New Military Humanism* and chapter 3, below.

23. For these and numerous other examples, see the references of note 4 and my *Year 501* (Boston: South End, 1993), *Powers and Prospects* (Boston: South End, 1996). *Inside Indonesia* (Australia), no. 62, April–June 2000. For Kurds, see chapter 1, p. 12; for Karnow and Valeriani, see also below.

24. Tyler Marshall, "Pentagon's Investment in Indonesia Lacks Payoff," *Los Angeles Times*, September 12 1999.

25. On the doctrines taught, see particularly Michael McClintock, *Instruments of Statecraft* (New York: Pantheon, 1992). On the remarkably consistent record of application, there is a rich literature: to

select only one example, Edward Herman, *The Real Terror Network* (Boston: South End, 1982). For careful review of one instructive category of cases, and the aftermath, see Thomas Walker and Ariel Armony, eds., *Repression, Resistance, and Democratic Transition in Central America* (Wilmington, Delaware: Scholarly Resources, 2000).

26. David Briscoe, AP Online, September 8 1999. On this and other exercises and training programs, see Alan Nairn, Statement to the US House of Representatives Subcommittee on Human Rights, May 11 2000 (*Peacework*, June 2000); Alan Nairn, *Our Kind of Guys: US and the Indonesian Military* (Verso, forthcoming).

27. Cited by Robert Cribb, ed., *The Indonesian Killings of 1965–1966* (Monash Papers on South-east Asia, no. 21, 1991). Estimates vary. Benedict Anderson believes that the toll may have reached over 2 million; "Petrus Dadi Ratu," *New Left Review*, 3, May–June 2000.

28. Brian Toohey and William Pinwill, *Oyster* (Port Melbourne: Heinemann, 1989), 93, censored by the Australian government. For review, see my *Year 501*, chapter 5.

29. McGeorge Bundy cited by David Fromkin and James Chace, *Foreign Affairs* (spring 1985). Robert McNamara, *In Retrospect* (New York: Times Books, 1995). Douglas Pike, *Viet Cong* (Cambridge MA: MIT Press, 1965). On McNamara's memoirs – remarkably, regarded by many opponents of the war as a "vindication" – see my "Memories," *Z magazine*, summer 1995; "Hamlet without the Prince," *Diplomatic History*, 20.3, summer 1996.

30. *Year 501*, chapter 7. For more extensive quotes and discussion, see my *On Power and Ideology* (Boston: South End, 1988).

31. John Andrews, "The Extended Family," *Economist*, August 15 1987; David Sanger, "Real Politics: Why Suharto Is In and Castro Is Out," *NYT*, October 31 1995. Nick Cohen, "Labour: quartermaster to tyranny in East Timor," *Observer*, September 5 1999. For more see *Year 501*, *Powers and Prospects*.

32. Reuters, "Indonesia Military Allowed To Obtain Training in U.S.," *NYT*, December 8 1993, a few lines on an inside page; Irene Wu, *Far Eastern Economic Review*, June 30 1994. See *Powers and Prospects* for further detail.

33. William Hartung, weapons specialist of the World Policy Institute, "Half an Island, Half a World Away," KRT News Service, September

16; John Donnelly, "Pentagon reluctant to isolate Indonesia," *BG* September 11 1999.

34. John Gittings, et al., "Cook faces new crisis as Hawk jets fly in," *Observer*, September 26; Robert Peston and Andrew Parker, "Public cash funded Indonesia Hawk sales," *Financial Times*, September 15; "Indonesia Air Force deploys Hawk fighter jets, radar in Kupang," BBC Summary of World Broadcasts, September 13, source 'Suara Pembaruan', Jakarta, in Indonesian, September 10 1999; Richard Norton-Taylor, "In the Swamp," *Guardian*, September 2 1999. Martyn Gregory, "World in Action," Granada production for ITV, June 2, 9, 1997. Ewen MacAskill, "Britain's ethical foreign policy: keeping the Hawk jets in action," *Guardian*, January 19 2000. On Britain's record, see John Taylor, *East Timor: The Price of Freedom* (London: Zed, 1999); and John Pilger, *Distant Voices* (London: Vintage 1992), *Hidden Agendas* (London: Vintage; New York: New Press, 1998).

35. Quoted by Pilger, ibid.

36. David Fromkin, *Kosovo Crossing* (New York: Free Press, 1999).

37. Hartung, op. cit. Ed Vulliamy and Antony Barnett, "US aided butchers of Timor," *Observer* (London, and foreign service), September 19; "US trained butchers of East Timor," *Guardian Weekly*, September 23 1999. A database search on September 29 found no mention in the US media.

38. Lansell Taudevin, *East Timor: Too Little, Too Late* (Potts Point NSW: Duffy & Snellgrove, 1999). Taudevin, who arrived in East Timor with "largely intact pro-Indonesian sentiments," ran an Australian aid project in East Timor from 1996 through March 1999, when he was expelled by Indonesia. Throughout this period he provided detailed reports of mounting Indonesian atrocities, known to Australian intelligence, conforming to Australian press reports, and well-confirmed in retrospect.

39. John Aglionby, et al., "Revealed: army's plot," *Observer*, September 12 (and foreign service); "For nearly a year, generals hatched murderous plan to block independence for East Timor – and Western intelligence services knew about it," *Globe and Mail* (Toronto), Observer Service, September 13 1999. No report was located in the US. Taudevin, op. cit. On Indonesian military and intelligence, see Richard Tanter, "East Timor and the Crisis of the Indonesian Intelligence State," in *Bulletin of Concerned Asian Scholars*, 32.1–2,

January–June 2000 and Richard Tanter, Mark Selden, and Stephen Shalom, eds., *East Timor, Indonesia, and the World Community* (Rowman & Littlefield, 2000); and Damien Kingsbury, "The TNI and the militias," in Kingsbury, ed., op. cit. For review and background, see Taylor, op. cit.

40. David Jenkins, Asia Editor, "Army's dirty tricks brigade unleashed in fight for Timor," *Sydney Morning Herald*, July 8 1999; Benedict Anderson, "Indonesian Nationalism Today and In the Future," *New Left Review*, 235, May/June 1999.

41. Taudevin, op. cit., who provides many details.

42. Andrew Fowler, "The Ties that Bind," Australian Broadcasting Corporation, February 14 2000.

43. Shenon, op. cit.

44. Taylor, op. cit., citing Church report of August 6; the report covers the period from January to mid-July. Taylor himself estimates the toll at 5–6,000 from January to the August 30 referendum. Arnold Kohen, "Beyond the Vote; The World Must Remain Vigilant Over East Timor," *WP*, September 5 1999. For review of the first part of the year, mainly from the Australian and British press, see *New Military Humanism.*

45. See Edward Herman and David Peterson, "How the New York Times Protects Indonesian Terror in East Timor," *Z magazine*, July/August 1999; and "East Timor: From 'Humanitarian' Bombing to Inhumane Appeasement," *CovertAction Quarterly*, fall–winter 1999.

46. Farhan Haq, "Rights–East Timor: U.N. Announces Delay in Vote," Inter Press Service, June 22 1999; "Indonesia–East Timor–US Senate Urges Clinton to Support Direct Ballots," Antara (Indonesian National News Agency), July 2 1999; David Shanks, "'Jakarta oligarchy' seen as hidden hand in strife," *Irish Times*, July 10 1999. M2 PRESSWIRE, July 8 1999, US Department of State daily press briefing.

47. Suratman cited by Brian Toohey, "Dangers of Timorese whispers capital idea," *Australian Financial Review*, August 14 1999, referring to a radio interview "earlier this year." Wayne Sievers, Andrew West, 'Timor action puts officer in firing line," *Sunday Age*, January 9 2000. Document, Aglionby, op. cit. A similar document, dated May 5 2000 is published in Human Rights Watch, *Forced Expulsions*. The Indonesian Investigative Commission for Human Rights Abuses in East Timor "confirmed the existence and validity of the Garnadi Document which ordered the burning of the troubled region" (*Indonesian*

Observer, January 4 2000), referring to a document, denied by the military, authorized from the highest levels of the military command.

48. Richard Lloyd Parry, "Conclusive proof TNI planned reign of terror," *Independent*, February 5 2000.

49. Mark Dodd, "Fears of bloodbath grow as militias stockpile arms," *Sydney Morning Herald*, July 26; Dennis Shanahan, "US was warned of militia link," *Australian*, September 24 1999.

50. Lindsay Murdoch, *The Age* (Australia), April 8; Barry Wain, Asia editor, *Wall Street Journal* (Asia edition), April 17 2000.

51. Alan Nairn, "US Complicity in Timor," *Nation*, September 27 1999; Nairn's testimony at hearings on the Humanitarian Crisis in East Timor, held before the International Operations And Human Rights Subcommittee of the US House Committee on International Relations on September 30 1999, in Washington, DC. See *Bulletin of Concerned Asian Scholars* and Tanter et al., note 39. Also references of note 26.

52. Elizabeth Becker, "U.S.-to-Jakarta Messenger: Chairman of the Joint Chiefs," *NYT*, September 14 1999. See notes 3, 24.

53. Sander Thoenes, "Martial law – Habibie's last card," *Financial Times*, September 8 1999; "What made Indonesia accept peacekeepers," *CSM*, September 14 1999. Shortly after, Thoenes was murdered in East Timor, apparently by TNI. See note 6.

54. Gay Alcorn, "'Too Late' to send armed UN force," *Sydney Morning Herald*, August 25 1999, citing State Department spokesman James Foley. Defense Secretary William Cohen, press briefing, September 8 1999.

55. Elizabeth Becker and Philip Shenon, "With Other Goals in Indonesia, U.S. Moves Gently on East Timor," *NYT*, September 9 1999. Steven Mufson, "West's Credibility at Stake, Laureate Says," *WP*, September 9 1999.

56. See chapter 1, pp. 30–31 for a few examples.

57. Peter Hartcher, "The ABC of winning US support," *Australian Financial Review*, September 13 1999.

58. Richard Butler, "East Timor: Principle v. Reality," *The Eye* (Australia), 7–20, 1999.

59. Daniel Southerland, "U.S. role in plight of Timor: an issue that won't go away," *CSM*, March 6 1980. See *Towards a New Cold War* for fuller quote and context.

60. *New York Times Magazine* writer James Traub, "Inventing East Timor," *Foreign Affairs*, July/August 2000.

61. Daniel Patrick Moynihan, with Suzanne Weaver, *A Dangerous Place* (Boston: Little, Brown, 1978). Moynihan writes that 60,000 were reported killed "since the outbreak of civil war." There had been a brief civil war, with 2–3,000 killed, months before the full-scale Indonesian invasion in December.

62. The only discussion prior to 1979, to my knowledge is in Arnold Kohen, "Human Rights in Indonesia," *Nation*, November 26 1977. The first journal article specifically dealing with East Timor may have been my "East Timor: the Press Cover-up," *Inquiry*, February 19 1979.

63. Stanley Karnow, Richard Valeriani, *Washington Journalism Review*, March 1980. A.J. Langguth, *Nation*, February 16 1980. For these and many other examples, see *Towards a New Cold War*, and for extensive review of the earlier record, Chomsky and Herman, *Political Economy of Human Rights*, the book Langguth was reviewing. Jean Daniel, editor, *Nouvel Observateur*, cited by Jean–Pierre Faye, *Change* (Paris), October 1979.

64. John Holdridge (State Department), Hearing before the Subcommittee on Asian and Pacific Affairs of the Committee on Foreign Affairs, House of Representatives, 97th Congress, 2nd session, September 14 1982, 71.

65. Binny Buchori and Sugeng Bahagijo, "The Case for Debt Relief," *Inside Indonesia*, January–March 2000. Karen Lissakers, *Banks, Borrowers, and the Establishment* (New York: Basic Books, 1991). For a lucid account of the role of the IMF, see Robin Hahnel, *Panic Rules!* (Cambridge: South End, 1999). On the interesting concept "debt," see my *Rogue States* (Cambridge: South End, 2000), chapter 8.

66. Audrey and George Kahin, *Subversion as Foreign Policy* (New York: New Press, 1995); *Powers and Prospects*. For details on the operations, see Kenneth Conboy and James Morrison, *Feet to the Fire: CIA Covert Operations in Indonesia, 1957–1958* (Annapolis: Naval Institute Press, 1999).

67. See sources cited earlier, and, for brief review, my "L'Indonésie," *Le Monde diplomatique*, June 1998.

68. Wm. Roger Louis, *Imperialism at Bay: The United States and the Decolonization of the British Empire, 1941–1945* (Oxford, 1978), 237.

CHAPTER THREE

Kosovo in Retrospect

The tumult having subsided, it should be possible to undertake a relatively dispassionate review and analysis of NATO's war over Kosovo. One might have expected the theme to have dominated the year-end millenarianism, considering the exuberance about a grand new era in human history that the war elicited in Western intellectual circles. But it received scant mention.

A rare exception was the *Wall Street Journal*, which devoted its lead story on December 31 to an in-depth analysis of what had taken place.[1] The headline reads: "War in Kosovo Was Cruel, Bitter, Savage; Genocide It Wasn't." The conclusion contrasts rather sharply with wartime propaganda. A database search of references to "genocide" in Kosovo for the first week of bombing alone was interrupted when it reached its limit of 1,000 documents.[2]

Hysterical exaggeration of the enemy's unfathomable evil is a classic feature of propaganda, particularly when it is recognized, at some level of awareness, that the case for resort to force is weak. The device is familiar in totalitarian states, but was pioneered in democracies, where the need to mobilize popular support is greater. World War I is a classic example; NATO's bombing campaign from March 24 1999 is another. Propaganda descended to a form of Holocaust revisionism, unusual in its prominence: right in the mainstream, not in despised and marginal sectors, a bitter insult to the memory of Hitler's victims. At first the focus was Milosevic personally. He was a second Hitler, threatening the very survival of civilization. When it became clear that the bombing was directed not against the Serb military but rather against the civilian society, it became necessary to shift grounds and demonize Serbs, "Milosevic's Willing Executioners" who deserved their fate and must be "cleansed" by the righteous avenger.[3] The authors, however, are not the "willing executioners" of the White House and its estimable clients, despite the relative ease with which they could confront terrible crimes, and the clear lesson of moral truisms.

As NATO forces entered Kosovo, tremendous efforts were undertaken to discover evidence of the enemy's crimes, a "model of speed and efficiency" to ensure that nothing would be lost or overlooked. The efforts "build on lessons learned from past mistakes." They reflect "a growing international focus on holding war criminals accountable." Furthermore, analysts add, "proving the scale of the crimes is also important to NATO politically, to show why 78 days of airstrikes against Serbian forces and infrastructure were necessary."[4]

The logic, widely accepted, is intriguing. Uncontroversially, the vast crimes took place after the bombing began: they were not a cause but – it is hard to deny – a consequence. Logic aside, it requires considerable audacity to take the crimes to provide retrospective justification for the actions that contributed to inciting them, even putting aside the fact that the consequence was anticipated.

One "lesson learned," and quickly applied, was the need to avoid a serious inquiry into the crimes then underway in East Timor, on a scale far beyond pre-bombing Kosovo. As discussed in chapter 2, in this case there was no "model of speed and efficiency." The US and Britain continued to support the crimes through their peak of fury in September 1999, refusing to allow any interference with the killers until international outrage became too intense to ignore. When the Indonesian military was at last directed to leave the country it had left in ruins, few forensic experts were sent despite the pleas of the UN peacekeeping mission, and those were delayed for many months, well after the rainy season would remove essential evidence. The mission itself was delayed even after the country had been virtually destroyed and most of its population expelled.

The distinction is not hard to comprehend. In East Timor, the crimes were attributable directly to state terrorists supported by the West. Accordingly, issues of accountability can hardly be on the agenda, and the "growing international focus on holding war criminals accountable" must quickly fade. In Kosovo, in contrast, evidence of terrible crimes can be adduced to provide retrospective justification for the NATO war, on the interesting principle that has been established by the doctrinal system.

Despite valiant efforts, the results of "the mass-grave obsession," as the *Wall Street Journal* analysts call it, were disappointingly thin. Instead of "the huge killing fields some investigators were led to expect, . . . the pattern is of scattered killings," a form of "ethnic cleansing light." "Most killings and burnings [were] in areas where the separatist Kosovo Liberation Army [KLA–UCK] had been active" or could infiltrate, some human rights researchers reported, an attempt "to clear out areas of KLA support, using selective terror, robberies and sporadic killings." These conclusions gain some support from the detailed report of the Organisation for Security and Co-operation in Europe (OSCE) released in December 1999, which "suggests a kind of military rationale for the expulsions, which were concentrated in areas controlled by the insurgents and along likely invasion routes."[5]

The *Wall Street Journal* analysts conclude that "NATO stepped up its claims about Serb 'killing fields'" when it "saw a fatigued press corps drifting toward the contrarian story: civilians killed by NATO's bombs" – and, much more significant, civilian infrastructure destroyed and war crimes, including chemical and biological warfare. If they are right, the change in the propaganda designed for the press corps mirrored the clear shift in home-front propaganda already mentioned. NATO spokesman Jamie Shea presented "information" that can be traced to KLA–UCK sources, and many of the most lurid and prominently-published atrocity stories attributed to refugees and other sources were untrue, the analysts conclude. Meanwhile, we discover elsewhere, NATO sought to deny its own atrocities, for example, by releasing a falsified videotape "shown at triple its real speed," to make it appear that "the killing of at least 14 civilians aboard a train on a bridge in Serbia last April" was unavoidable because "the train had been traveling too fast for the trajectory of the missiles to have been changed in time."[6] Fabrication of enemy crimes and suppression of one's own are, again, familiar and expected features of wartime propaganda, particularly when "contrarian stories" begin to surface.

The *Wall Street Journal* analysts nevertheless believe that the "heinous" crimes committed by Serbia, including the huge campaign of expulsion, "may well be enough to justify" the NATO bombing campaign, on the principle of retrospective justification crafted by the doctrinal system.

The December 1999 OSCE review was the third major source to become available concerning Serb crimes. The first was the State Department's detailed case against Milosevic and his associates in May 1999; the second, their formal indictment shortly after by the International Tribunal on War Crimes. The two sources are very similar, presumably because the "remarkably fast indictment" by the Tribunal was based on US–UK "intelligence and other information long denied to [the Tribunal] by Western governments." Few expect that such information would be released for a war crimes tribunal on East Timor. The State Department updated its case in December 1999, presenting what it described as the definitive justification for the bombing, including whatever information could be obtained from refugees and investigations after the war.[7]

In the two State Department reports and the Tribunal indictment, the detailed chronologies are restricted, almost entirely, to the period that followed the bombing campaign initiated on March 24 1999. Thus, the final State Department report of

December 1999 refers vaguely to "late March" or "after March," apart from a single reference to refugee reports of an execution on March 23, two days after the air operations had been announced, a day after NATO's official declaration that they were about to begin.[8] The State Department is therefore instructing us, in the clearest terms, that the crimes of "Milosevic's willing executioners" were not a motive for the bombing: the crimes followed the bombing, according to the State Department's definitive case against Milosevic, and were precipitated by it, it is only rational to assume.

The one significant exception is the January 15 1999 Racak massacre of forty-five people. But that cannot have been the motive for the bombing, for two sufficient reasons: first, the OSCE monitors and other international observers (including NATO) report this to be an isolated event, with nothing similar in the following months up to the bombing; we return to that record directly. And second, such atrocities are of little concern to Washington and its allies. Evidence for the latter conclusion is overwhelming, and it was confirmed once again shortly after the Racak massacre, when Indonesian forces and their paramilitary subordinates brutally murdered dozens of people – or perhaps many more – who had taken refuge from Indonesian terror in a church in the Timorese village of Liquica twenty miles from the capital city of Dili, known at once though not investigated, and reported only meagerly. Unlike Racak, this was only one of many massacres in East Timor at that time. The US and its allies reacted to the East Timor massacres in the familiar way: by continuing to provide military and other aid to the killers, maintaining military relations and proceeding with joint military exercises, while protecting them from international interference.[9]

In summary, the State Department and the Tribunal make no serious effort to justify the bombing campaign or the withdrawal of the OSCE monitors (Kosovo Verification Mission, KVM) on March 20 in preparation for it.

The OSCE inquiry conforms closely to the indictments produced by the State Department in May and December and by the Tribunal. It records "the pattern of the expulsions and the vast increase in lootings, killings, rape, kidnappings and pillage once the NATO air war began on March 24."[10] "The most visible change in the events was after NATO launched its first airstrikes" on March 24, the OSCE reports. "On one hand, the situation seemed to have slipped out of the control of any authorities, as lawlessness reigned in the form of killings and the looting of houses. On the other, the massive expulsion of thousands of residents from the city, which mostly took place in the last week of March and in early April, followed a certain pattern and was conceivably organized well in advance."[11]

The word "conceivably" is surely an understatement. Even without documentary evidence, one can scarcely doubt that Serbia had plans for expulsion of the population, and would be likely to put them into effect under NATO bombardment, with the prospect of direct invasion. It is commonly argued that the bombing is justified by the plans that were implemented in response to the bombing. Again, the logic is interesting. Adopting the same principle, terrorist attacks on US targets would be justified if they elicited a nuclear attack, in accord with plans – which exist – for first strike, even pre-emptive strike against non-nuclear states that have signed the non-proliferation treaty.[12] Similarly, an Iranian missile attack on Israel with a credible invasion threat would be justified if Israel responded by implementing its plans – which presumably exist – for expelling the Palestinian population. The implications of the thesis, if taken seriously, are impressive.[13]

The OSCE reports further that "Once the OSCE–KVM [monitors] left on 20 March 1999 and in particular after the start of the NATO bombing of the FRY [Federal Republic of Yugoslavia] on 24 March, Serbian police and/or VJ [Yugoslav army], often accompanied by paramilitaries, went from village to village and, in the towns, from area to area threatening and expelling the Kosovo Albanian population."[14] The departure of the monitors also precipitated an increase in KLA–UCK ambushes of Serbian police officers, "provoking a strong reaction" by police, an escalation from "the pre-war atmosphere, when Serbian forces were facing off against the rebels, who were kidnapping Serbian civilians and ambushing police officers and soldiers."[15]

"Indiscriminate attacks on populated areas, sporadic prior to 24 March 1999, became a widespread occurrence after that date," the OSCE reports. "There was a pattern of targeting people who had or were perceived to have UCK [KLA] connections," which "might have led to arrest" before the March 20 withdrawal of the monitors, though "after that date the intentions of the Yugoslav and Serbian forces were more likely to be murderous." "The level of incidents of summary and arbitrary killing escalated dramatically immediately after the OSCE–KVM withdrew on 20 March"; two incidents are described on the 20th, another more serious one on the 24th. Next is: "further escalation after 24 March 1999. Summary and arbitrary killing became a generalized phenomenon throughout Kosovo with the beginning of the NATO air campaign against the FRY on the night of 24–25 March."

"Up to that point [March 24]," the OSCE review continues, "the attentions of the Yugoslav and Serbian military and security forces had been generally directed towards communities in Kosovo in areas that were on UCK transit routes or where there were UCK bases . . . After 24 March however the general pattern changed and included areas that had previously been relatively quiet." "The areas that were under the influence of the UCK or of strategic importance were among the first to be targeted simultaneously on 24 March, and continued to be targeted for some time thereafter."[16]

"By March 1999, the Yugoslav military/security forces were coping with two tasks: defeating the UCK and preparing for an attack by NATO," directing "resources and attention" primarily "to the west of Kosovo and the border with Albania," where there "existed not only a possible route for NATO to enter, but an area where the UCK was particularly active, with 'safe havens' and supplies in Albania [which] would be in a position to reach other UCK zones further into Kosovo if the military/security forces were not able to dominate the ground in the area." The first priority of the Yugoslav forces was "securing the lines of communication," and controlling villages lying along strategic routes," which "were immediately shelled and cleared," along with those "lying at important crossroads":

While combating the UCK in the hills and villages, the security forces later attempted to deny the UCK their base of support including non-military supplies. In effect, this meant the forced displacement of Kosovo Albanians from villages in known UCK areas and the pursuit of IDPs [internally displaced persons] in the hills, particularly the targeting of men of fighting age. Operations in the east consisted of establishing and building up VJ [army] defences, starting from the border and moving further into Kosovo.[17]

In brief, by March 1999 the Serbian authorities were responding much as would be expected in the face of the threat of bombing and perhaps invasion by the global superpower and its allies, in support of Albania-based guerrilla forces operating in the province that Washington insists is part of Serbia.

According to Albanian Kosovar legal adviser Marc Weller, a strong advocate of the bombing, "within a few days [after the withdrawal of the monitors on March 20], the number of displaced had again risen to over 200,000," figures that conform roughly to US intelligence reports.[18] Then came the bombing, and the huge escalation of atrocities and expulsions.

For an understanding of NATO's resort to war, the most important period is the months leading up to the decision. And of course, NATO's perception of what was happening during that period is a matter of critical significance for any serious attempt to evaluate the decision to bomb Yugoslavia without Security Council authorization. Fortunately, that is the period for which we have the most detailed direct evidence: namely, from the reports of the KVM monitors and other international observers. Unfortunately, the OSCE inquiry passes over these months quickly, presenting little evidence and concentrating rather on the period after monitors were withdrawn; and the State Department (and Tribunal) virtually ignore the crucial period. A selection of KVM reports is, however, available, along with others by NATO and independent international observers.[19] These merit close scrutiny. The relevant period begins in December, with the breakdown of the cease-fire that had permitted the return of many people displaced by the fighting.[20] Throughout these months, the monitors report that "humanitarian agencies in general have unhindered access to all areas of Kosovo," with occasional harassment from Serb security forces and KLA paramilitaries, so the information may be presumed to be fairly comprehensive.

Before reviewing this material, let us look back to the immediate context.

Kosovo had been an extremely ugly place in the preceding year. About 2,000 were killed according to NATO, mostly Albanians, in the course of a bitter struggle that began in February 1998 with attacks on Serb police and civilians by well-armed KLA guerrillas based in Albania that the US denounced as "terrorism," and a brutal Serb response. By summer the KLA had taken over about 40 per cent of the province, eliciting a vicious reaction by Serb security forces and paramilitaries, targeting civilians alleged to be supporting the guerrillas. In September, the UN Security Council demanded a cease-fire and negotiations, and an agreement between the KLA and Serbia was brokered by US envoy Richard Holbrooke, followed by dispatch of KVM monitors. The agreement "had come just in time for the guerrillas," Tim Judah writes. They "were hard pressed and were holed up in the hills," and the agreement gave them "a reprieve, time to reorganise and rearm, and, as they told anyone who cared to listen, time to prepare for their spring [1999] offensive."[21]

The KLA was also telling anyone who cared to listen about their tactics and the reasons for them. US intelligence warned that the KLA "intended to draw NATO into its fight for independence by provoking Serb atrocities." The KLA was arming and "taking very provocative steps in an effort to draw the West into the crisis," hoping for a brutal Serb reaction, Holbrooke later commented.[22]

On December 8 1998, the Foreign Ministers of the European Union "expressed concern for the 'recent intensification of military action' in Kosovo, noting that increased activity by the KLA has prompted an increased presence of Serbian security forces in the region." The KLA were "the main initiators of violence . . . [in] . . . a deliberate campaign of provocation," the North Atlantic Council had concluded shortly before, a conclusion endorsed in internal deliberations by US Ambassador William Walker, who headed the KVM. The reasons for the campaign were explained by KLA and other Albanian Kosovar leaders: "any armed action we undertook would bring retaliation against civilians," and "the more civilians were killed, the chances of intervention became bigger," as brutal and well-publicized Serb reactions aroused Western support for military intervention. "We knew full well that any armed action we undertook would trigger a ruthless retaliation against our people," KLA leader Hashim Thaci informed BBC investigators, referring to the killing of four Serb policemen a week before the Racak massacre: "We knew we were endangering civilian lives, too, a great number of lives." "It was guaranteed that every time we took action they would take revenge on civilians," another KLA fighter said, describing the killing of the policemen that led to the Serb attack on Racak, which was "a ferocious struggle" in which both sides "suffered heavy losses," Thaci reports. "As top KLA military commander Agim Ceku boasted, . . . [the KLA] . . . shared in the 'victory' because 'after all, the KLA brought NATO to Kosovo'" by carrying out attacks, which the US labelled "terrorist," in order to elicit violent retaliation.[23]

The British press reports further that CIA officers acting under the cover of the KVM have admitted giving covert assistance to the KLA in planning such armed actions, targeting Serb police and civilians. One CIA agent commented that "I'd tell them which hill to avoid, which wood to go behind, that sort of thing." "European diplomats then working for the OSCE claim it was betrayed by an American policy that made airstrikes inevitable."[24]

British Defence Minister Lord George Robertson, later NATO Secretary-General, informed the House of Commons as the bombing began that until mid-January 1999, "the KLA were responsible for more deaths in Kosovo than the Yugoslav authorities had been"[25] – which implies that the same was roughly true up to the bombing on March 24, if we can believe the rich documentation provided by US government and other Western sources. Robertson is referring to the period before the Racak massacre of January 15, in which forty-five were reported killed. That single case aside, Western documentation (as distinct from public commentary) indicates no changes of significance in the ten weeks that followed. Hence, if Lord Robertson's report to Parliament were correct, it would follow that the assignment of responsibility for killing is about the same up to the bombing. Given the relative scale of the military forces involved, Robertson's estimate is not credible, but it does give a useful insight into the perceptions of those who launched the bombing.

Recognizing the likely consequences, NATO planners were concerned about how the public would react after a few days of airstrikes, "when the first images of humanitarian suffering and probably Serb revenge slaughter of Albanians start hitting the TV news bulletins." But as of March 20 (when the KVM monitors were withdrawn in preparation for bombing), their prime concern appears to have been that "NATO's credibility will be destroyed if it dithers indefinitely and fails to deliver on its threats," though they recognized that, "[t]here are never military solutions to difficult political problems" such as those of Kosovo.[26] As we have seen, concern for "NATO's credibility" was a principal if not the leading concern throughout.

Let us turn to the documentary review of the crucial period from December 1998 to the withdrawal of the monitors and the bombing on March 24 1999.

The "most serious incidents" reported by the ICRC in December are clashes along the FRY–Albanian border, and "what appear to be the first deliberate attacks on public places in urban areas." The UN Inter-Agency Update of December 24 identifies these as an attempt by armed Albanians to cross into Kosovo from Albania, leaving at least thirty-six armed men dead, and the killing of six Serbian teenagers by masked men spraying gunfire in a cafe in the largely Serbian city of Pec. The next incident is the abduction and murder of the Deputy Mayor of Kosovo Polje, attributed by NATO to the KLA–UCK (p. 327). Then follows a report of "abductions attributed to the KLA." The UN Secretary-General's report on December 24 reviews the same evidence, citing the figure of 282 civilians and police abducted by the KLA as of December 7 (FRY figures).

The general picture is that after the October cease-fire, "Kosovo Albanian paramilitary units have taken advantage of the lull in the fighting to re-establish their control over many villages in Kosovo, as well as over some areas near urban centres and highways, . . . leading to statements [by Serbian authorities] that if the [KVM] cannot control these units the government would." Recall that this is the conclusion reached by the EU Foreign Ministers and the North Atlantic Council at the same time.

The UN Inter-Agency Update on January 11 is similar. It reports fighting between Serb security forces and the KLA. In addition, in "the most serious incident since the declaration of the cease-fire in October 1998, the period under review has witnessed an increase in the number of murders (allegedly perpetrated by the KLA), which have prompted vigorous retaliatory action by government security forces." "Random violence" killed twenty-one people in the preceding eleven days. Only one example is cited: a bomb outside "a cafe in Pristina, injuring three Serbian youths and triggering retaliatory attacks by Serbian civilians on Albanians," the first such incident in the capital. The other major incidents cited are KLA capture of eight soldiers, the killing of a Serbian civilian, and the reported killing of three Serbian police. NATO's review of the period is similar, with further examples: VJ shelling of civilian and UCK facilities with "at least 15 Kosovo Albanians" killed; UCK killing of a Serb judge, police and civilians; and others.

Then comes the Racak massacre of January 15, after which the reports return pretty much to what preceded. The OSCE monthly report of February 20 describes the situation as "volatile." Serb–KLA "direct military engagement . . . dropped significantly," but KLA attacks on police and "sporadic exchange of gunfire" continued, "including at times the use of heavy weapons by the VJ." The "main feature of the last part of the reporting period has been an alarming increase in urban terrorism with a series of indiscriminate bombing or raking gunfire attacks against civilians in public places in towns throughout Kosovo"; these are "non-attributable," either "criminally or politically motivated." Then follows a review of police–KLA confrontations, KLA abduction of "five elderly Serb civilians," and refusal of KLA and VJ to comply with Security Council resolutions. Five civilians were killed as "urban violence increased significantly," including three killed by a bomb outside an Albanian grocery store. "More reports were received of the KLA 'policing' the Albanian community and administering punishments to those charged as collaborators with the Serbs," also KLA murder and abduction of alleged Albanian collaborators and Serb police. The "cycle of confrontation can be generally described" as KLA attacks on Serb police and civilians, "a disproportionate response by the FRY authorities," and "renewed KLA activity elsewhere."

In his monthly report of March 17, the UN Secretary-General reports that clashes between Serb security forces and the KLA "continued at a relatively lower level," but civilians "are increasingly becoming the main target of violent acts," including killings, executions, mistreatment, and abductions. The UNHCR "registered more than 65 violent deaths" of Albanian and Serb civilians (and several Roma) from January 20 to March 17. These are reported to be isolated killings by gunmen and grenade attacks on cafes and shops. Victims included alleged Albanian collaborators and "civilians known for open-mindedness and flexibility in community relations." Abductions continued, the victims almost all Serbs, mostly civilians. The OSCE report of March 20 gave a similar picture, reporting "unprovoked attacks by the KLA against the police" and an increase in casualties among Serb security forces, along with "Military operations affecting the civilian population," "Indiscriminate urban terrorist attacks targeting civilians," "non-attributable murders," mostly of Albanians, and abduction of Albanian civilians, allegedly by a "centrally-controlled" KLA "security force." Specific incidents are then reported.

The last NATO report (January 16–March 22) cites several dozen incidents, about half initiated by KLA–UCK, half by Serb security forces, in addition to half a dozen responses by Serb security forces and engagements with the KLA, including "Aggressive Serb attacks on villages suspected of harbouring UCK forces or command centres." Casualties reported are mostly military, at the levels of the preceding months.

As a standard of comparison, one might consider the regular murderous and destructive US-backed Israeli military operations in Lebanon when Israeli forces occupying southern Lebanon in violation of Security Council orders, or their local mercenaries, were attacked by the Lebanese resistance. Through the 1990s, as before, these have far exceeded anything attributed to the FRY security forces within what NATO insists is their territory.

Within Kosovo, no significant changes are reported from the breakdown of the cease-fire in December until the March 22 decision to bomb. Even apart from the (apparently isolated) Racak massacre, there can be no doubt that the FRY authorities and security forces were responsible for serious crimes. But the reported record lends no credibility to the claim that these were the reason for the bombing; in the case of comparable or much worse atrocities during the same period, the US and its allies either did not react, or – more significantly – maintained and even increased their support for the atrocities. Examples are all too easy to enumerate: East Timor in the same months, to mention only the most obvious one.

The Racak massacre was quickly seized upon by advocates of bombing as the event they had been waiting for. Secretary of State Madeleine Albright called National Security Adviser Sandy Berger to tell him that "Spring has come early to Kosovo," referring presumably to the planned spring offensive that the KLA had been describing to "anyone who cared to listen." "Racak transformed the West's Balkan policy as singular events seldom do," *Washington Post* correspondent Barton Gellman observed in reconstructing "the path to crisis." This was the "Defining Atrocity" that "Set Wheels in Motion," the headline reads. Albright is reported to have been "outraged by the massacre," but if true, that is a severe indictment, considering her reaction to massacres to which she actively contributes; the same is true of others who do not react far more energetically to massacres for which they share responsibility.[27]

Albright recognized at once that Racak "clearly is a galvanising event and we had to move the Allies as rapidly as we could." She was "quick to grasp that the atrocity could be used with great effect to stiffen international resolve" against Milosevic. All doubts about what happened were quickly set aside, along with what was known about the tactic of provoking massacres to elicit NATO intervention, Racak included.[28]

I know of only one other record from official Western sources, namely, documents from Germany's Foreign Ministry and German Courts.[29]

On January 12 1999, Foreign Office Intelligence reported that "[e]ven in Kosovo an explicit political persecution linked to Albanian ethnicity is not verifiable. The East of Kosovo is still not involved in armed conflict. Public life in cities like Pristina, Urosevac, Gnjilan, etc. has, in the entire conflict period, continued on a relatively normal basis." The "actions of the security forces [were] not directed against the Kosovo-Albanians as an ethnically defined group, but against the military opponent and its actual or alleged supporters."

On February 4, an Administrative Court hearing asylum requests concluded that from May to July 1998, Foreign Office status reports "do not allow the conclusion that there is group persecution of ethnic Albanians from Kosovo . . . The violent actions of the Yugoslav military and police since February 1998 were aimed at separatist activities and are no proof of a persecution of the whole Albanian ethnic group in Kosovo or in a part of it." These actions were "a selective forcible action against the military underground movement (especially the KLA) and people in immediate contact with it in its areas of operation . . . A state program or persecution aimed at the whole ethnic group of Albanians exists neither now nor earlier."

Citing status reports of the Foreign Office, the Upper Administrative Court of Münster concluded on February 24 that reports agree "that the often feared humanitarian catastrophe threatening the Albanian civil population has been averted," after "the winding down of combat in connection with an agreement made with the Serbian leadership at the end of 1998 . . . Since that time both the security situation and the conditions of life of the Albanian-derived population have noticeably improved . . . Specifically in the larger cities public life has since returned to relative normality." The court found that :"[t]here is no sufficient actual proof of a secret program, or an unspoken consensus on the Serbian side, to liquidate the Albanian people, to drive it out or otherwise to persecute it in the extreme manner presently described . . . Events since February and March 1998 do not evidence a persecution program based on Albanian ethnicity. The measures taken by the armed Serbian forces are in the first instance directed toward combatting the KLA and its supposed adherents and supporters."

On March 11, the same court held that "[e]thnic Albanians in Kosovo have neither been nor are now exposed to regional or countrywide group persecution in the Federal Republic of Yugoslavia." On March 15, Intelligence reported that "As laid out in the status report of November 18, 1998, the KLA has resumed its positions after the partial withdrawal of the (Serbian) security forces in October 1998, so it once again controls broad areas in the zone of conflict. Before the beginning of spring 1999 there were still clashes between the KLA and security forces, although these have not until now reached the intensity of the battles of spring and summer 1998."

The documentary sources available agree that prior to the bombing, even after the withdrawal of the monitors, the situation remained fairly stable, with KLA actions (possibly with CIA involvement) designed to elicit a violent and disproportionate Serbian response, which rarely failed to come, and was exploited eagerly by the advocates of bombing to mobilize Western opinion for their cause.

The vast expulsions from Kosovo began immediately after the March 24 bombing campaign. On March 27, the UNHCR reported that 4,000 had fled Kosovo, and on April 1, the flow was high enough for UNHCR to begin to provide daily figures. Its Humanitarian Evacuation Programme began on April 5. From the last week of March to the end of the war in June, "forces of the FRY and Serbia forcibly expelled some 863,000 Kosovo Albanians from Kosovo," the OSCE reports, and hundreds of thousands of others were internally displaced, while Serbs, Roma and others fled as well.

Former *New York Times* Balkans specialist David Binder notes "a curiosity" documented in the OSCE report: 46 per cent of Albanians left Kosovo during the bombing, along with 60 per cent of Serbians and Montenegrins. Thus, "proportionately more Serbs were displaced during the bombing, and they did not return to Kosovo." They were followed later by many other non-Albanians under the eyes of the NATO occupying forces, who "have far outstripped everyone else in ethnic cleansings in the Balkans."[30]

The US and UK had been planning the bombing campaign for many months, and could hardly have failed to anticipate these consequences. In early March, Italian Prime Minister Massimo D'Alema warned Clinton of the huge refugee flow that would follow the bombing; Clinton's National Security Adviser Sandy Berger responded that in that case "NATO will keep bombing," with still more horrific results. US intelligence also warned that there would be "a virtual explosion of refugees" and a campaign of ethnic cleansing, reiterating earlier predictions of European monitors.[31]

As the bombing campaign began, US-NATO Commanding General Wesley Clark informed the press that it was "entirely predictable" that Serb terror would intensify as a result. Shortly after, Clark explained again that "[t]he military authorities fully anticipated the vicious approach that Milosevic would adopt, as well as the terrible efficiency with which he would carry it out." Elaborating a few weeks later, he observed that the NATO operation planned by "the political leadership . . . was not designed as a means of blocking Serb ethnic cleansing. It was not designed as a means of waging war against the Serb and MUP [internal police] forces in Kosovo. Not in any way. There was never any intent to do that. That was not the idea." As already noted General Clark stated further that he had not been informed of the alleged Serb plan to expel the population (Operation Horseshoe) that had been publicized by Germany after the shocking Serb reaction to the bombing had become evident, and has become a staple since, despite its dubious origins.[32]

The agency that bears primary responsibility for care of refugees is UNHCR. "At the war's end, British Prime Minister Tony Blair privately took the agency to task for what he considered its problematic performance."[33] Evidently, the performance of UNHCR would have been less problematic had the agency not been defunded by the great powers. For this reason, the UNHCR had to cut staff by over 15 per cent in 1998. In October, while the bombing plans were being formulated, the UNHCR announced that it would have to eliminate a fifth of its remaining staff by January 1999 because of the budgetary crisis created by the new generation.[34]

In summary, the KVM monitors were removed and a bombing campaign initiated with the expectation, quickly fulfilled, that the consequence would be a sharp escalation of ethnic cleansing and other atrocities, after the organization responsible for care of refugees was defunded. Under the doctrine of retrospective justification, the heinous crimes that ensued are now held to be, perhaps, "enough to justify" the NATO bombing campaign.

The person who commits a crime bears the primary responsibility for it; those who incite him, anticipating the consequences, bear secondary responsibility, which only mounts if they act to increase the suffering of the victims. The only possible argument for action to incite the crimes is that they would have been even more severe had the action not been undertaken. That claim, one of the most remarkable in the history of support for state violence, requires substantial evidence. In the present case, one will seek evidence in vain – even recognition that it is required, or comprehension of what it entails.[35]

Suppose, nevertheless, that we take the argument seriously. It plainly loses force to the extent that the subsequent crimes are great. If no Kosovar Albanians had suffered as a result of the NATO bombing campaign, the decision to bomb might be justified on the grounds that crimes against them might have been deterred. The force of the argument diminishes as the scale of the crimes increases. It is, therefore, rather curious that supporters of the bombing seek to portray the worst possible picture of the crimes for which they share responsibility; the opposite should be the case. The odd stance presumably reflects the success in instilling the doctrine that the crimes incited by the NATO bombing provide retrospective justification for it.

This is by no means the only impressive feat of doctrinal management. Another is the debate over NATO's alleged "double standards" and "inconsistency," revealed by its "looking away" from other humanitarian crises, or "doing too little" to prevent them, or "tolerating" abuses and "failing to protect" the victims. Participants in the debate must be agreeing that NATO was guided by humanitarian principles in Kosovo – precisely the question at issue. That aside, the Clinton Administration did not "tolerate" or "look away" from atrocities in Turkey, East Timor, Colombia, or many other places, but rather chose to escalate them, along with its allies, often vigorously and decisively, facts that remain stubbornly invisible to those who share responsibility for these crimes and prefer to focus their outrage in a different direction.

It is a rare achievement for a propaganda system to have its doctrines adopted as the very presuppositions of debate. These are among the "lessons learned," to be applied in future exercises cloaked in humanitarian intent, as often before.

The absurdity of the principle of retrospective justification is, surely, recognized at some level. Accordingly, many attempts to justify the NATO bombing take a different tack. One typical version is that "Serbia assaulted Kosovo to squash a separatist Albanian guerrilla movement, but killed 10,000 civilians and drove 700,000 people into refuge in Macedonia and Albania. NATO attacked Serbia from the air in the name of protecting the Albanians from ethnic cleansing [but] killed hundreds of Serb civilians and provoked an exodus of tens of thousands from cities into the countryside."[36] Assuming that order of events, a rationale for the bombing can be constructed. But uncontroversially, the actual order is the opposite. The device is common in the media, and scholarship often adopts a similar stand, as already illustrated.

Such revision of the factual record has been standard procedure throughout. In a typical earlier version, *New York Times* foreign policy specialist Thomas Friedman wrote at the war's end that "once the refugee evictions began, ignoring Kosovo would be wrong . . . and therefore using a huge air war for a limited objective was the only thing that made sense."[37] The refugee evictions to which he refers followed the "huge air war," as anticipated. Again, the familiar inversion, which is understandable: without it, defense of state violence becomes difficult indeed.

One commonly voiced retrospective justification is that the resort to force made it possible for Kosovar Albanians to return to their homes. "The West can be proud of its role in ending terror and mass expulsions from Kosovo," the editors of the *New York Times* concluded. Discussing the great success of the war he supervised, former Secretary-General of NATO Javier Solana wrote that

> with no casualties of its own, NATO had prevailed. A humanitarian disaster had been averted. About one million refugees could now return to safety. Ethnic cleansing had been reversed.

A significant achievement, if we overlook the actual order of events. By this reasoning, a preferable alternative – grotesque, but less so than the policy pursued – would have been to induce Kosovar Albanians to leave peacefully and with proper care, then to bomb the FRY to ensure their return, having suffered far less harm than they did when expelled under NATO's bombs.

Another retrospective justification, also commonly invoked, is that even before the bombing, murderous ethnic cleansing was underway. Recall the official version of the Clinton Administration, reiterated in January 2000: "on March 21, the day after the withdrawal of the Kosovo Verification Mission (KVM) monitors, Serb forces "launched a major offensive," "dubbed 'Operation Horseshoe'." In another variant, Cambridge University Law Professor Marc Weller, in his Introduction to the volume of documents on Kosovo that he edited, recognizes that the NATO bombing, which he strongly supported, is in clear violation of international law, and might be justified only on the basis of an alleged "right of humanitarian intervention." That justification rests in turn on the assumption that the FRY refusal "to accept a very detailed settlement of the Kosovo issue [the Rambouillet ultimatum] would constitute a circumstance triggering an overwhelming humanitarian emergency." But events on the ground "relieved NATO of having to answer this point," he writes: namely, "the commencement of a massive and pre-planned campaign of forced deportation of what at one stage seemed to be almost the entire ethnic Albanian population of Kosovo just before the bombing campaign commenced."[38]

As discussed, this device faces a few problems. First, the documentary record provides no evidence for the crucial factual claim, and indeed refutes it (given the absence of evidence despite extensive efforts to unearth it); that includes the US government records presented as the definitive justification of the bombing and the volume Weller edited. Second, even if it had been discovered later that the expulsion had commenced before the bombing, that could hardly justify the resort to force, by simple logic; and as just discussed, even if the commencement of the expulsion had been known before the bombing (though mysteriously missing from the documentary record), it would have been far preferable to allow the expulsion to proceed, and then to initiate the bombing to ensure the return of those expelled: grotesque, but far less so than what was undertaken. Third, NATO Commander Clark denied that NATO had plans to impede the ethnic cleansing that he regarded as an "entirely predictable" consequence of the bombing as it began, and also had no knowledge of Operation Horseshoe, if the plan even exists. Fourth, even if an undocumented "major offensive" had been launched after the withdrawal of the monitors in preparation for the bombing, that would hardly justify these NATO decisions. But in the light of the evidence available, all of this is academic, merely an indication of the desperation of the efforts to justify the war.

Were less grotesque options available in March 1999? The burden of proof, of course, is on those who advocate state violence; it is a heavy burden, which there has been no serious attempt to meet. But let us put that aside, and look into the range of options available.

An important question, raised by journalist Eric Rouleau, is whether "Serbian atrocities had reached such proportions as to warrant breaking off the diplomatic process to save the Kosovars from genocide." He observes that "[t]he OSCE's continuing refusal to release the report [on the observations of the KVM monitors from November until their withdrawal] can only strengthen doubts about the truth of that allegation."[39] As noted earlier, the State Department and Tribunal indictments provide no meaningful support for the allegation – not an insignificant fact, since both sought to develop the strongest case. What about the OSCE report, released since Rouleau wrote? As discussed, the report makes no serious effort to support the allegation, indeed provides little information about the crucial period. Its references in fact confirm the testimony of French KVM member Jacques Prod'homme, which Rouleau cites, that "in the month leading up to the war, during which he moved freely throughout the Pec region, neither he nor his colleagues observed anything that could be described as systematic persecution, either collective or individual murders, burning of houses or deportations."

The detailed reports of KVM and other observers omitted from the OSCE review undermine the allegation further, as already discussed.

The crucial allegation remains unsupported, though it is the central component of NATO's case, as even the most dedicated advocates recognize, Marc Weller for example. And once again, it should be stressed that a heavy burden of proof lies on those who put it forth to justify the resort to violence. The discrepancy between what is required and the evidence presented is quite striking; the term "contradiction" would be more apt, particularly when we consider other pertinent evidence, such as the direct testimony of the military commander.

Suppose the monitors had not been withdrawn in preparation for the bombing, and diplomatic efforts had been pursued. Were such options feasible? Would they have led to an even worse outcome, or perhaps a better one? Since NATO refused to entertain this possibility, we cannot know. But we can at least consider the known facts, and ask what they suggest.

Could the KVM monitoring team have been left in place, preferably strengthened? That seems possible, particularly in the light of the immediate condemnation of the withdrawal by the Serb National Assembly. No argument has been advanced to suggest that the reported increase in atrocities after their withdrawal would have taken place even had they remained, let alone the vast escalation that was the predicted consequence of the bombing signalled by the withdrawal. NATO also made little effort to pursue other peaceful means; even an oil embargo, the core of any serious sanctions regime, was not considered until after the bombing.

The most important question, however, has to do with the diplomatic options. Two proposals were on the table on the eve of the bombing. One was the Rambouillet accord, presented to Serbia as an ultimatum. The second was Serbia's position, formulated in its March 15 "Revised Draft Agreement" and the Serb National Assembly Resolution of March 23.[40] A serious concern for protecting Kosovars might well have brought into consideration other options as well, including, perhaps, something like the 1992–93 proposal of the Serbian President of Yugoslavia, Dobrica Cosic, that Kosovo be partitioned, separating itself from Serbia apart from "a number of Serbian enclaves."[41] At the time, the proposal was rejected by Ibrahim Rugova's Republic of Kosovo, which had declared independence and set up a parallel government; but it might have served as a basis for negotiation in the different circumstances of early 1999. Let us, however, keep to the two official positions of late March: the Rambouillet ultimatum and the Serb Resolution.

It is important and revealing that, with marginal exceptions, the essential contents of both positions were kept from the public eye, apart from dissident media that reach few people.

The Serb National Assembly Resolution, though reported at once on the wire services, has remained a virtual secret. There has been little indication even of its existence, let alone its contents. The Resolution condemned the withdrawal of the OSCE monitors and called on the UN and OSCE to facilitate a diplomatic settlement through negotiations, "toward the reaching of a political agreement on a wide-ranging autonomy for [Kosovo], with the securing of a full equality of all citizens and ethnic communities and with respect for the sovereignty and territorial integrity of the Republic of Serbia and the Federal Republic of Yugoslavia." It raised the possibility of an "international presence" of a "size and character" to be determined to carry out the "political accord on the self-rule agreed and accepted by the representatives of all national communities living in [Kosovo]." The FRY agreement "to discuss the scope and character of international presence in [Kosovo] to implement the agreement to be accepted in Rambouillet" had been formally conveyed to the negotiators on February 23, and announced by the FRY at a press conference the same day.[42] Whether these proposals had any substance we cannot know, since they were never considered, and remain unknown.

Perhaps even more striking is that the Rambouillet ultimatum, though universally described as *the* peace proposal, was also kept from the public, particularly the provisions "tacked on late in the negotiations, that would have given NATO troops the freedom to operate anywhere in Yugoslavia" (Barry Posen) – a "killer clause" that entailed "a loss of sovereignty that was clearly unacceptable," Michael MccGwire comments, requiring Milosevic to "allow NATO to use Serbia as a part of the NATO organization" (Lord Carrington, former NATO Secretary-General, then Chair of the Hague Peace Conference for Yugoslavia).[43] Though much remains obscure, it appears that these provisions were introduced after Serbia had expressed agreement with the main political proposals, and virtually guaranteed Serbia's rejection of the package. The "killer clause" to which Lord Carrington and strategic analysts refer is the section of the implementation appendices that accords NATO the right of "free and unrestricted passage and unimpeded access throughout the FRY including associated airspace and territorial waters," without limits or obligations or concern for the laws of the country or the jurisdiction of its authorities, who are, however, required to follow NATO orders "on a priority basis and with all appropriate means" (Appendix B).

The annex containing these provisions was kept from journalists covering the Rambouillet and Paris talks, Robert Fisk reports. "The Serbs say they denounced it at their last Paris press conference – an ill-attended gathering at the Yugoslav Embassy at 11pm on March 18." Serb dissidents who took part in the negotiations allege that they were given these conditions on the last day of the Paris talks, and that the Russians did not know about them. The annex was not made available to the British House of Commons until April 1, the first day of the Parliamentary recess, a week after the bombing started.[44]

In the negotiations that began after the bombing, NATO abandoned these demands entirely, along with others to which Serbia had been opposed, and there is no hint of them in the final peace agreement. Fisk asks: "What was the real purpose of NATO's last minute demand? Was it a Trojan horse? To save the peace? Or to sabotage it?" Whatever the answer, if the NATO negotiators had been concerned with the fate of the Kosovar Albanians, they would have sought to determine whether diplomacy could succeed if NATO's most provocative, and evidently irrelevant, demands had been withdrawn; and the monitoring enhanced, not terminated.

In his attempt to reconstruct NATO reasoning, MccGwire concludes that "the available evidence supports the widespread impression that Rambouillet was set up to fail," not only because of the "killer clause," but also because of "the studied avoidance of any reference to the UN and the insistence that the operation would be solely under NATO auspices, NATO-led and NATO-manned." The fate of the latter demands is instructive. In the final peace accords of June, and the Security Council Resolution confirming them, these demands too were abandoned, at least formally, though the US made it clear at once that it would ignore the documents it had signed and reinstate the Rambouillet terms that had been officially dropped.

If the "killer clause" was "a drafting error" that was not intended seriously, as was later claimed, then "this could have been easily corrected," MccGwire observes, "so it is fair to assume that the inclusion of this obviously unacceptable condition was deliberate." The conclusion is supported by Britain's second most senior defence minister during the war, Lord Gilbert, defence minister of state formally responsible for intelligence. Testifying before the Defence Select Committee, "he claimed that allied forces forced Slobodan Milosevic into a war." "I think certain people were spoiling for a fight in NATO at that time," he informed the Committee. "I think the terms put to Milosevic at Rambouillet were absolutely intolerable: how could he possibly accept them? It was quite deliberate." MccGwire suggests that the reason may have been "the importance of demonstrating the continuing relevance of the [NATO] alliance on its fiftieth anniversary, and the opportunity presented by the Kosovo crisis to further the out-of-area issue and to establish NATO's right to act without specific UN endorsement," exactly the "opportunity" condemned outside the self-designated "international community," at the time and since. Another goal, he suggests, was the "urge to punish and humiliate Milosevic" for his recalcitrance. These considerations fall within the doctrinal sense of "credibility of NATO," as already discussed.[45]

In the doctrinal sense, "credibility of NATO" means "credibility of the US." "Washington's preference for force" and in particular Albright's "saber-rattling" had irritated other NATO countries in the build-up to the bombing, though "US officials were unapologetic about the hard line."[46] MccGwire also discusses US preference for NATO rather than "the OSCE route," with its priority for diplomacy rather than force; the European role is sharply reduced when a confrontation is moved to the arena of violence, where the US reigns supreme and where its British associate too enjoys its comparative advantage. Transfer of the issue to NATO virtually ensures that outcome. Neither diplomacy nor a "less threatening" implementation force "would have been acceptable to the United States," MccGwire comments, in part because of US distaste for multilateralism and its hostile relations to the UN, but also because it "was - determined to prevent the emergence of an alternative Europe-wide security structure that could challenge its authority." Washington's objective was "to demonstrate NATO's continuing utility and future potential" while "showing off NATO's political muscle." Carrots were dismissed in favor of sticks, he writes, and "the longer-term and more important objective of avoiding civil war had to yield precedence to the immediate requirement to bolster NATO credibility by punishing Milosevic for taking issue with its demands" – another warning to the "disorderly elements of the world," one may add.[47]

When questions have been raised about the "killer clause" and other exorbitant demands, leaders of the US and UK negotiating teams have claimed that they were willing to drop these provisions, but that the Serbs refused. The claim is hardly credible. If it were true, there would have been every reason for the US and Britain to have made such facts public at once. Nor does the claim account for the fact that the demands that critics describe as "clearly unacceptable" (MccGwire) were recognized by NATO to be unnecessary, and quickly withdrawn after the bombing commenced.

Prominent advocates of the bombing have made similar claims. An important example is the commentary on Rambouillet by Marc Weller.[48] Weller ridicules the "extravagant claims" about the implementation appendices, which he says were "published along with the agreement," meaning the Draft Agreement dated February 23 – which may be technically accurate, in a very narrow sense of "published," but misses the point. Plainly, they were highly significant. It is therefore necessary to explain why outstanding reporters covering the Rambouillet and Paris talks were unaware of them; or, it appears, the British Parliament. The "famous Appendix B," Weller states, established "the standard terms of a status of forces agreement for KFOR [the planned NATO occupying forces]." "True, but misleading," MccGwire observes: "The issue was one of geographical scope and, by UN procedure, the appendix should have applied to Kosovo only and not the whole Federal Republic"[49] – as indeed it did, with NATO acquiescence, having been dropped by NATO after the bombing began and conceded to be of no importance for the forces that entered Kosovo in June 1999. These forces are far larger than what was contemplated at Rambouillet and therefore should be even more dependent on the status of forces agreement. Also unexplained is the March 15 FRY response to the February 23 Draft Agreement. The FRY response goes through the Draft Agreement in close detail, section by section, proposing extensive changes and deletions throughout, but includes no mention at all of the appendices – the implementation agreements, which, Weller points out, were by far the most important part and were the subject of the Paris negotiations then underway. One can only view his account with some skepticism. For the moment, these important matters remain buried in considerable obscurity.

The documents were available to any news media that chose to pursue the matter. In the US, the extreme (and plainly irrelevant) demand for virtual NATO occupation of the FRY received its first mention at a NATO briefing of April 26, when a question was raised about it but was quickly dismissed and not pursued. The facts were, however, reported as soon as the demands had become irrelevant to public awareness and democratic choice. Immediately after the announcement of the peace accords of June 3, the press quoted the crucial passages of the "take it or leave it" Rambouillet ultimatum, noting that they required that "a purely NATO force was to be given full permission to go anywhere it wanted in Yugoslavia, immune from any legal process," and that "NATO-led troops would have had virtually free access across Yugoslavia, not just Kosovo."[50]

Through the seventy-eight days of bombing, negotiations continued, each side making compromises – described in the US as Serb deceit, or capitulation under the bombs. The peace agreement of June 3 was a compromise between the two positions on the table in late March. NATO abandoned its most extreme demands, including those that had apparently undermined the negotiations at the last minute and the wording that had been interpreted as calling for a referendum on independence. Serbia agreed to an "international security presence with substantial NATO participation," the sole mention of NATO in the peace agreement or Security Council Resolution 1244 affirming it. As noted, NATO had no intention of living up to the scraps of paper it had signed, and moved at once to violate them, implementing a military occupation of Kosovo under NATO command and castigating Serbia and Russia for their deceit when they insisted on the terms of the formal agreements, so that bombing was renewed to bring them to heel. The media and most commentators fell into line with scarcely a hint of possible impropriety, following longstanding precedents. Again conforming to precedent, the matter has disappeared from history, the norm within the most powerful state when it chooses to disregard mere formalities, such as the agreements it has accepted.[51]

While Serbia and Russia were deceitfully insisting on the terms of the official agreements, NATO planes disciplined them by again bombing the oil refineries in Novi Sad and Pancevo, both centers of opposition to Milosevic, on June 7. The Pancevo refinery burst into flames, releasing a huge cloud of toxic fumes, shown in a photo accompanying a *New York*

Times story of July 14, which discussed the severe economic and health effects. The bombing itself was not reported, though it was covered by wire services.[52]

It has been argued that Milosevic would have tried to evade the terms of an agreement, had one been reached in March. The record strongly supports that conclusion, just as it supports the same conclusion about NATO – not only in this case; forceful dismantling of formal agreements is the norm on the part of the great powers.[53] As now belatedly recognized, the record also suggests that "it might have been possible [in March] to initiate a genuine set of negotiations – not the disastrous American diktat presented to Milosevic at the Rambouillet conference – and to insert a large contingent of outside monitors capable of protecting Albanian and Serb civilians alike."[54]

At least this much seems clear. NATO chose to reject diplomatic options that were not exhausted, and to launch a military campaign that had awful consequences for Kosovar Albanians, as anticipated. Other consequences are of little concern in the West, including the devastation of the civilian economy of Serbia by military operations that severely violate the laws of war.

The matter was brought to the International Criminal Tribunal for the Former Yugoslavia (ICTY) during the war, but it will not be addressed, the Tribunal has announced, even the massive criminal attack on civilian infrastructure in an effort to terrorize the population, or such individual incidents as NATO's bombing of Serbian state TV and radio killing sixteen journalists on grounds that it was "a facility used for propaganda purposes," as the Pentagon put it in its review of the air campaign, after NATO spokesperson David Wilby had stated that it would not be bombed if it broadcast six hours of Western news a day. The Tribunal did regard it as "controversial" to justify the attack on TV and radio "on the propaganda purpose to which it was employed," citing Wilby's statement and others. But it nevertheless chose to accept the NATO justification in terms of "dual use" capability of radio and TV (which could be used for military communications). The Committee to Protect Journalists refused to list the Serb victims in its annual report of murdered journalists, on grounds that they are propagandists, not journalists. Monitors of media independence accepted this judgment without comment.[55]

The Tribunal also stoutly defends its independence. Others, however, might tend to heed the words of NATO spokesman James Shea, when asked about the possibility of NATO liability in news conferences in May 1999. He replied that "NATO is the friend of the Tribunal . . . NATO countries are those that have provided the finances to set up the Tribunal, we are among the majority financiers." He was "certain" that the Prosecutor would only indict "people of Yugoslav nationality."[56]

For similar reasons, there is little likelihood that the Tribunal will pay attention to its 150-page "Indictment Operation Storm: A Prima Facie Case," reviewing the war crimes committed by Croatian forces that drove some 200,000 Serbs from Krajina in August 1995 with crucial US involvement that elicited "almost total lack of interest in the US press and in the US Congress," *New York Times* Balkans correspondent David Binder observes.[57]

The suffering of Kosovars did not end with the arrival of the

NATO (KFOR) occupying army and the UN mission. Though billions of dollars were readily available for bombing, five months after the war ended the US had not paid any of the $37.9 million assessed for the start-up costs of the United Nations civilian operation. By November, "the US Office of Foreign Disaster Assistance has yet to distribute any heavy-duty kits and is only now bringing lumber" for the winter shelter program in Kosovo; the UNHCR and EU humanitarian agency ECHO have also "been dogged with criticism for delays and lack of foresight." The current shortfall for the UN mission is "the price of half a day's bombing," an embittered senior UN official said, and without it "this place will fail," to the great pleasure of Milosevic. A November donors' conference of Western governments pledged only $88 million to cover the budget of the UN mission in Kosovo, but pledged $1 billion in aid for reconstruction for the next year – public funds that will be transferred to the pockets of private contractors, if there is some resolution of the controversies within NATO about how the contracts are to be distributed. In mid-December the UN mission again pleaded for funds for teachers, police officers and other civil servants, to little effect. Three months later the head of the UN Mission described it as "barely alive." In July 2000, the House and Senate Appropriations Committees "rejected a request for $107 million for current expenses in Kosovo and East Timor."[58]

Washington is even refusing to allow US weapons disposal experts to remove the thousands of unexploded cluster bombs scattered over Kosovo, anti-personnel weapons that are far more lethal than landmines: "The job is being dumped

on underfunded civilian teams, largely staffed by Albanians."
The New Zealand colonel heading the UN civilian demining
team observed that "NATO doesn't want to create a precedent for cleaning up in post-conflict situations." Over fifty
people had been killed by unexploded cluster bombs from
the war's end until March 2000, with a mounting toll expected
over the summer when farmers and children return to the
fields.[59]

In July 1995, Milan Martic, President of the self-declared
Serb Republic in Croatia, was indicted by the ICTY for having
ordered a missile attack on Zagreb in retaliation for a Croatian
offensive that drove many Serbs from their homes, killing seven
civilians. It was a war crime, the ICTY determined, because the
missiles were fitted with cluster bombs, and such a device "is an
anti-personnel weapon designed only to kill people," hence
prohibited against civilian targets. The Pentagon reported that
"American planes dropped 1,100 cluster bomb canisters, with
220,000 bomblets, over Kosovo," while "British planes dropped
about 500 bombs, each with 147 bomblets." Cluster bombs were
also used in attacking civilian targets in Serbia, for example in
a May 7 attack on the city of Nis, killing fifteen people in the
market and also hitting the city's main hospital. But these are
not crimes, just "mistakes made by NATO," the ICTY Prosecutor
informed the Security Council.[60]

Despite the limited post-war aid, the appeal of a disaster
that can be attributed to an official enemy, and exploited (on
curious grounds) "to show why 78 days of airstrikes against
Serbian forces and infrastructure were necessary," has been
sufficient to bring severe cutbacks in aid elsewhere. The US

Senate planned to cut tens of millions of dollars from Africa-related programs. Denmark reduced non-Kosovo assistance by 26 per cent. International Medical Corps was compelled to suspend its Angola program, having raised $5 million for Kosovo while it hunts, in vain, for $1.5 million for Angola, where 1.6 million displaced people face starvation. The World Food Program announced that it would have to curtail its programs for 2 million refugees in Sierra Leone, Liberia, and Guinea, having received less than 20 per cent of requested funding. The same fate awaits 4 million starving people in Africa's Great Lakes region – whose circumstances are not unrelated to Western actions over many years, and refusal to act at critical moments. UNHCR expenditures per refugee in the Balkans are eleven times as high as in Africa. "The hundreds of millions of dollars spent on Kosovo refugees and the crush of aid agencies eager to spend it 'was almost an obscenity,' said Randolph Kent," who moved from UN programs in the Balkans to East Africa. President Clinton held a meeting with leading aid agencies "to emphasize his own enthusiasm for aid to Kosovo."[61]

All of this is against the background of very sharp reductions in aid in the United States, now "at the height of its glory" (Fromkin), the leadership basking in adulation for their historically unprecedent "altruism" as they virtually disappear from the list of donors to the poor and miserable.

The OSCE inquiry provides a detailed record of crimes committed under NATO military occupation. Though these do not begin to compare with the crimes committed by Serbia under NATO bombardment, they are not insignificant. The occupied province is filled with "lawlessness that has left violence unchecked," much of it attributed to the KLA–UCK, the OSCE reports, while "impunity has reigned instead of justice." Albanian opponents of the "new order" under "UCK dominance," including officials of the "rebel group's principal political rival," have been kidnapped, murdered, targeted in grenade attacks, and otherwise harassed and ordered to withdraw from politics. The one selection from the OSCE reports in the *New York Times* concerns the town of Prizren, near the Albanian border. It was attacked by Serbs on March 28, but "the overall result is that far more damage has been caused . . . after the war than during it." British military police report involvement of the Albanian mafia in grenade attacks and other crimes, along with such acts as murder of elderly women by "men describing themselves as KLA representatives."[62]

The Serb minority has been largely expelled. Robert Fisk reports that "the number of Serbs killed in the five months since the war comes close to that of Albanians murdered by Serbs in the five months before NATO began its bombardment in March"; recall that the UN reported "more than 65 violent deaths" of civilians (Albanian and Serb primarily) in the two months before the withdrawal of the monitors and the bombing. Murders are not investigated, even the murder of a Serb employee of the International Tribunal. The Croat community "left en masse" in October. In November, "the President of the tiny Jewish community in Pristina, Cedra Prlincevic, left for Belgrade after denouncing 'a pogrom against the non-Albanian population'." Amnesty International reported at the year's end that "Violence against Serbs, Roma,

Muslim Slavs and moderate Albanians in Kosovo has increased dramatically over the past month," including "murder, abductions, violent attacks, intimidation, and house burning . . . on a daily basis," as well as torture and rape, and attacks on independent Albanian media and political organizations in what appears to be "an organized campaign to silence moderate voices in ethnic Albanian society," all under the eyes of NATO forces.[63]

The fate of the Roma is particularly grim, as throughout Europe. The Roma International Center in Macedonia alleges that "more than 120,000 Kosovo Roma have sought refugee [status] in Europe, while 20–30,000 are living under extreme conditions in the enclaves in Kosovo." The *Voice of Roma* in Italy, reviewing the situation in detail, concludes that the reason why "Roma are overlooked is because they are completely irrelevant to the explicit and implicit goals of the Western powers, whereas the other groups of 'political refugees' support, encourage, and embrace the Westernization of the former Yugoslavia." Thousands were forced to flee from Kosovo to Italy at gunpoint under the NATO occupation, many dying when ships sink. "Most Romani neighborhoods in Kosovo have been burned and destroyed, with a few of the nicer houses left intact, now occupied by Albanians in front of the eyes of KFOR forces and UNHCR." Conditions in the Italian refugee camps are "appalling." "Humanitarian assistance, help and protection of Roma in and from Kosovo has been and continues to be virtually nonexistent." A Roma historian from Pristina describes how his house was burned, his sister raped, and his neighbor kidnapped by ethnic Albanians, while his relatives and friends were taken to KLA torture chambers, all with the knowledge of KFOR forces who tell them "it's OK." Like many Roma refugees, he was able to flee by bribing the Albanian mafia.[64]

KFOR officers report that their orders are to disregard crimes: "Of course it's mad," a French commander said, "but those are the orders, from NATO, from above." NATO forces also "seem completely indifferent" to attacks by "armed ethnic Albanian raiders" across the Serb-Kosovo border "to terrorize border settlements, steal wood or livestock, and, in some cases, to kill," leaving towns abandoned. Former KLA fighters are pursuing the strategy they used in Kosovo earlier. "By ordering the ambushing of Serbian police officers and sometimes the intimidation of Serbian farmers, the leaders of this new army 'are hoping that the Serbs will retaliate with excessive force against civilian populations and create a wave of outrage and pressure on KFOR to respond', said a United Nations official." Ambushes of Serb police and "attacks on more moderate or loyal Albanian politicians in Serbia have also increased." A US colonel said: "The concern here isn't that the Serbian police will come across, but that Albanian attacks on Serb police and army will inspire a response great enough to cause public clamor for a KFOR response," once again.[65]

Current indications are that Kosovo under NATO occupation is reverting to what was developing in the early 1980s, after the death of Tito, when nationalist forces undertook to create an "ethnically clean Albanian republic," taking over Serb lands, attacking churches, and engaging in "protracted violence" to attain the goal of an "ethnically pure" Albanian region, with "almost weekly incidents of rape, arson, pillage and industrial sabotage, most seemingly designed to drive Kosovo's remaining indigenous Slavs . . . out of the province." This "seemingly intractable" problem, another phase in an ugly history of intercommunal violence, led to Milosevic's characteristically brutal response, withdrawing Kosovo's autonomy and the heavy federal subsidies on which it depended, and imposing an "Apartheid" regime (Vickers).[66] Kosovo may also come to resemble Bosnia, "a den of thieves and tax cheats" with no functioning economy, dominated by "a wealthy criminal class that wields enormous political influence and annually diverts hundreds of millions of dollars in potential tax revenue to itself."[67] Much worse may be in store as independence for Kosovo becomes entangled in pressures for a "greater Albania," with dim portents.

The entrenchment of organized crime in Kosovo has reportedly led to an increase in trafficking of drugs and women, sold to Albanian pimps who "work under the protection of major crime figures in Kosovo, officials said, including some with links" to the KLA, a new problem in post-war Kosovo. An Italian specialist describes "the Albanians as particularly ferocious. In three or four years in the biggest Italian cities they have succeeded in destroying the competition of the other organizations. Albanians scare the Sicilian mafia," which had in any event shunned the sexual slave trade, now expanding rapidly.[68]

UN Special Investigator for the former Yugoslavia Jiri Dienstbier reported to the UN Commission on Human Rights that "330,000 Serbs, Roma, Montenegrins, Slavic Muslims, pro-Serb Albanians and Turks had been displaced in Kosovo – double the earlier estimates. What that means is most of Kosovo's minorities no longer are in their original homes." "The Yugoslav economy was destroyed. Kosovo is destroyed. There are hundreds of thousands of people unemployed now," he said. "There is a very general pessimism." Bitterly critical of NATO policy during and since the war, the former Czech dissident and post-Communist Foreign Minister also warned that Milosevic's position in Serbia might become stronger "unless the Kosovo situation changes and anti-Serbian sanctions are lifted."[69]

The poorer countries of the region have incurred enormous losses from the blocking of the Danube by NATO bombing at Novi Sad, another center of opposition to Milosevic. They were already suffering from protectionist barriers that "prevent the ships from plying their trade in the EU," as well as "a barrage of Western quotas and tariffs on their exports." But "blockage of the [Danube] is actually a boon" for Western Europe, particularly Germany, which benefits from increased activity on the Rhine and at Atlantic ports.[70]

There are other winners. At the war's end, the business press described "the real winners" as Western military industry, meaning high-tech industry generally. Moscow is looking forward to a "banner year for Russian weapons exports" as "the world is rearming apprehensively largely thanks to NATO's Balkans adventure," seeking a deterrent, as widely predicted during the war.[71] More important, the US was able to enforce its domination over the strategic Balkans region, displacing EU initiatives at least temporarily, very likely a primary reason for the insistence that the operation be in the hands of NATO, a US subsidiary. A destitute Serbia remains the last hold out, probably not for long.

A further consequence is another blow to the fragile principles of world order. The NATO action represents a threat to the "very core of the international security system" founded on the UN Charter, Secretary-General Kofi Annan observed in his annual report to the UN in September 1999.[72] That matters little to the rich and powerful, who will act as they please, rejecting World Court decisions and vetoing Security Council resolutions if that is deemed necessary; it is useful to remember that, contrary to much mythology, the US has been far in the lead in vetoing Security Council resolutions on a wide range of issues, including terror and aggression, ever since it lost control of the UN in the course of decolonization, with Britain second and France a distant third. But the traditional victims take these matters more seriously, as the global reaction to the Kosovo war indicated, and more recently the South Summit.

The essential point, not very obscure, is that the world faces two choices with regard to the use of force: (1) some semblance of world order, either the UN Charter or something better if it can gain a degree of legitimacy; or (2) the powerful states do as they wish unless constrained from within, guided by interests of power and profit, as in the past. It makes good sense to struggle for a better world, but not to indulge in pretense and illusion about the one in which we live.

Archival and other sources should provide a good deal more information about the latest Balkans war. Any conclusions reached today are at best partial and tentative. As of now, however, the "lessons learned" do not appear to be particularly attractive.

Notes

1. Daniel Pearl and Robert Block, *Wall Street Journal* (henceforth *WSJ*), December 31 1999.
2. David Peterson, personal communication; search of NEXIS database in All-News category.
3. For examples, and the transition, see *New Military Humanism* (henceforth *NMH*).
4. Scott Peterson, "This time, war-crimes trail is on a fast track," *Christian Science Monitor*, August 27 1999.
5. Steven Erlanger, "Monitors' Reports Provide Chronicle of Kosovo Terror," *New York Times* (henceforth *NYT*), December 5 1999.
6. AP, "NATO used speeded-up film to excuse civilian deaths in Kosovo," January 6 2000, citing *Frankfurter Rundschau*, January 6.
7. US Department of State, "Erasing History: Ethnic Cleansing in Kosovo," State Department website, http://www.state.gov/index.html, May 1999. Roger Cohen, Jane Perlez, *NYT*, May 28 1999, with two full pages devoted to "key sections." US Department of State, "Ethnic Cleansing in Kosovo: An Accounting," December 1999: http://www.state.gov/www/global/human_rights/kosovoii/intro. html. On the May 1999 documents, see *NMH*.
8. Marc Weller, ed., *International Documents & Analysis*, vol. 1, *The Crisis in Kosovo 1989–1999* (Cambridge UK: Documents & Analysis Publishing, Cambridge University Press, 1999), 495.
9. See chapter 2.
10. Erlanger, op. cit.
11. Ibid., from OSCE, *KOSOVO/KOSOVA As Seen, As Told* (henceforth *OSCE*), V: The municipalities, for Pristina/Prishtina city.
12. On Clinton era plans and Presidential Directives to implement them, see *NMH*, chapter 6; *The Defense Monitor*, XXIX.3, 2000.
13. The Serbian case is different, it is sometimes argued, because of

Milosevic's earlier crimes. On this remarkable and very revealing stand, see chapter 1, pp. 37f.

14. *OSCE*, part III: The violation of human rights in Kosovo (chapter 14).

15. Erlanger, op. cit., citing *OSCE*.

16. *OSCE*, part I, October 1998 to June 1999 (chapter 5).

17. *OSCE*, part II: The military/security context (chapter 3).

18. Marc Weller, "The Rambouillet Conference," *International Affairs*, 75.2, April 1999.

19. Weller, *International Documents*. The documents in this useful collection should be distinguished from the commentary, which is often thinly disguised advocacy of his clients and the bombing by the editor. A few examples appear below.

20. Ibid., 313–46.

21. Tim Judah, *Kosovo: War and Revenge* (New Haven: Yale University Press, 2000), 178ff.

22. Ibid.

23. EU General Affairs Council, reported in *Agence Europe*, no. 7559, December 9 1998, 4; cited by Peter Gowan, *The Twisted Road to Kosovo* (Oxford: Labour Focus on Eastern Europe, 1999). Alan Little, "Moral Combat: NATO At War," BBC2 Special, March 12 2000, and "How Nato was sucked into Kosovo conflict," *Sunday Telegraph* (London), February 27 2000. Agim Ceku, see Lenard Cohen, "Kosovo: 'Nobody's Country'," *Current History*, March 2000. A former brigadier in the Croatian army, US-trained, Ceku is under investigation by the International War Crimes Tribunal for his role in ethnic cleansing and atrocities from 1993–95 in Krajina, the site of the worst single ethnic cleansing operation of the Balkans war in 1995, conducted with US assistance and probably direct participation. Tom Walker, "Kosovo defence chief accused of war crimes," *Sunday Times* (London), October 10 1999; John Sweeney and Jens Holsoe, *Observer*, March 12 2000. On Krajina, see *NYT* Balkans correspondent David Binder, "The Role of the United States in the Krajina issue," *Mediterranean Quarterly*, 1997.

24. Tom Walker and Aidan Laverty, "CIA aided Kosovo guerrilla army," *Sunday Times*, March 12 2000.

25. House of Commons Select Committee on Defence, Minutes of Evidence, Examination of Witnesses (Questions 380–399), March

24 1999, Rt. Hon. George Robertson, MP. Also cited by MccGwire, "Why did we bomb Belgrade?" op. cit.

26. Report on the "New NATO" session, March 20 1999, "in the style of a memo" to Prime Minister Tony Blair and German Chancellor Gerhard Schroeder; Tim Judah, op. cit., 235ff.

27. Albright, Judah, op. cit., 194. Barton Gellman, "The Path to Crisis: How the United States and Its Allies Went to War; The Battle for Kosovo, A Defining Atrocity Set Wheels in Motion," *International Herald Tribune* (henceforth *IHT*), April 23 1999.

28. Little, op. cit.; see pp. 105f., above. On the doubts, see Judah, Little, op. cit.

29. Important Internal Documents from Germany's Foreign Office, at http://www.suc.org/kosovo_crisis/documents/ger_gov.html. Translated by Eric Canepa, Brecht Forum, New York, April 28 1999. Excerpts were obtained by IALANA (International Association of Lawyers Against Nuclear Arms), which distributed them to the press; these are from *Junge Welt*, April 24 2000. The court cases involve asylum claims, which might suggest "a bias in favor of downplaying a humanitarian catastrophe in order to limit refugees," Canepa notes, but "it nevertheless remains highly significant that the Foreign Office, in contrast to its public assertion of ethnic cleansing and genocide in justifying NATO intervention, privately continued to deny their existence as Yugoslav policy in this crucial period," into March 1999.

30. *OSCE* part III (chapter 14). Carlotta Gall, *NYT*, April 5 1999. Binder, "Why the Balkans?," *Blaetter fuer deutsche und internationale Politik*, May 2000.

31. For sources, see *NMH*.

32. Ibid., citing General Wesley Clark, "Overview," *NYT*, March 27 and *Sunday Times* (London), March 28; *Newsweek*, April 12; BBC, "Panorama: War Room," April 19 1999. On Operation Horseshoe, see chapter 1, pp. 34f.

33. Elizabeth Becker, "Military Leaders Tell Congress of NATO Errors in Kosovo," *NYT*, October 15 1999.

34. Frances Williams et al., *Financial Times*, October 7 1998.

35. See chapter 1, pp. 37f.

36. Daniel Williams, "No Exit for the Chechens," *IHT–Washington Post* (henceforth *WP*) Service, October 30 1999.

37. *NYT*, June 4 1999.

38. *International Documents*, 33.
39. Eric Rouleau, *Le Monde diplomatique*, December 1999.
40. On the first, see *International Documents*, 480ff. On both, and on media coverage, see *NMH*, 106ff.
41. Miranda Vickers, *Between Serb and Albanian: A History of Kosovo* (New York: Columbia University Press, 1998).
42. See *NMH*, 108ff, for further details; *International Documents*, 470; Mark Littman, *Kosovo: Law and Diplomacy*, Centre for Policy Studies, London, November 1999.
43. Barry Posen, "The War for Kosovo," *International Security*, 24.4, spring 2000; MccGwire, op. cit.
44. Robert Fisk, *Independent*, November 26 1999; Littman, op. cit.
45. MccGwire, op. cit. Patrick Wintour, "War strategy ridiculed," *Guardian*, July 21; Reuters, "British minister slams Kosovo war strategy," *Financial Times*, July 21 2000.
46. Kevin Cullen, "U.S., Europeans in Discord over Kosovo," *Boston Globe* (henceforth *BG*), February 22 1999.
47. MccGwire, op. cit.; see chapter 1, pp. 7–8, 41–2.
48. Weller, *International Documents*, 411. As noted, the commentaries are barely-concealed advocacy.
49. MccGwire, op. cit.
50. Steven Erlanger, *NYT*, June 5; Blaine Harden, *NYT*, same day, oblique reference; Guy Dinmore, *Financial Times*, June 6 1999. See *NMH* for further details.
51. See *NMH*, 114ff, 124ff, for review and precedents.
52. Wire services, June 7, 8 1999. Chris Hedges, "Serbian Town Bombed by NATO Fears Effects of Toxic Chemicals," *NYT*, July 14 1999. Also *Los Angeles Times* (henceforth *LA Times*), July 6 1999.
53. See *NMH* 124ff, on the recent US record.
54. Editorial, "Kosovo without illusions," *BG*, December 9 1999.
55. Barbara Crossette, "U.N. War Crimes Prosecutor Declines to Investigate NATO," *NYT*, June 3 2000. On NATO crimes, see Amnesty International, *NATO/Federal Republic of Yugoslavia: 'Collateral Damage' or Unlawful Killings*, June 2000; Robert Fisk, "Nato 'deliberately attacked civilians in Serbia'," *Independent*, June 7; Steven Erlanger, "Rights Group Says NATO Bombing in Yugoslavia Violated Law," June 8 2000. For a careful review of the Tribunal's exemption of NATO from crimes that often duplicate or magnify

those of local people indicted and sentenced, see Robert Hayden, "Biased 'Justice': Humanrightsism and the International Criminal Tribunal for the Former Yugoslavia," ms., University of Pittsburgh, February 2000. David Wilby, TV-radio, see Amnesty International, Hayden. Final Report to the Prosecutor by the Committee Established to Review the NATO Bombing Campaign Against the Federal Republic of Yugoslavia. Committee to Protect Journalists, see Hayden; James Boylan, "Book Reports," *Columbia Journalism Review* May/June 2000. On the Tribunal generally, see also Christopher Black and Edward Herman, *Z magazine*, February 2000.

56. James Shea, May 16, 17, cited by Hayden, op. cit.
57. David Binder, "The Role of the United States in the Krajina Issue," op. cit. (note 23). On the leaked and forgotten indictment, see Ray Bonner, "War Crimes Panel Finds Croat Troops 'Cleansed' the Serbs," *NYT*, March 21 1999.
58. *NYT*, October 6; Carlotta Gall, "Thousands of Kosovars, After Many Pledges, Still Await Winter Aid," *IHT–NYT*, November 3; Steven Erlanger, *NYT*, November 23, and Barbara Borst, "Retired officers pushing to aid Serbian cities,' *BG*, October 19; AP, "UN official begs for aid for mission in Kosovo," *BG*, December 17 1999. Steven Erlanger, "U.N.'s Kosovo Chief Warns that Mission is 'Barely Alive'," *NYT*, March 4 2000. Barbara Crossette, "Washington Takes a Blast from Its Envoy At the U.N.," *NYT*, July 21 2000. The Committees also cut the total budget request for peacekeeping in 2001 from $738 to $500, and the US stalled action on a Security Council resolution to expand peacekeeping operations in Sierra Leone, sponsored by Britain in response to a recommendation by Kofi Annan.
59. Jonathan Steele, "U.S. Refuses to remove cluster bombs in Kosovo," *Guardian*, March 14 2000.
60. Hayden, op. cit. Crossette, *NYT*, June 3 2000.
61. John Donnelly, "Relief agencies see Kosovo aid causing shortfall elsewhere," *BG*, July 8; Christian Miller and Ann Simmons, *L.A. Times*, May 21; Karen DeYoung, "U.S. Grows Stingier on Foreign Aid," *IHT–WP*, November 26 1999.
62. Jeffrey Smith, "Actions Louder Than Words," *WP Weekly*, December 13; *NYT*, December 5; Peter Beaumont, "Albanian mafia wages war on Kosovo's Serbs," *Guardian*, August 19 1999.

63. Robert Fisk, "Serbs murdered by the hundred since 'liberation'," *Independent*, November 24 1999. Interview with Cedra Prlincevic, http://www.emperors-clothes.com, November 1999. Amnesty International News Release, December 23 1999.
64. "Declaration: The Kosovo Conflict and the Consequences on the Roma initiated by the Kosovo Conflict," Skopje, June 16–18 2000. "Romani Refugees from Kosovo and the Bigger Picture of Humanitarian Aid Organizations Operation in Europe," *Voice of Roma*, Italian Mission, 1999; September 17–October 7 1999.
65. Tim Judah, "Kosovo: Peace Now?," *New York Review*, August 21; Robert Block, "Old Hates Reignite and Blood Flows at Kosovo Border," *WSJ*, December 17 1999. Carlotta Gall, *NYT*, January 15; Steven Erlanger, "Kosovo Rebels Regrouping Nearby in Serbia," *NYT*, March 2 2000.
66. Marvine Howe, "Exodus Of Serbians Stirs Province In Yugoslavia," *NYT*, July 12; David Binder, "Yugoslavs Seek To Quell Strife In Region Of Ethnic Albanians," *NYT*, November 9; Binder, "War Of Terror By Albanians In Yugoslavia Strains Unity," November 28 1982. Binder, "In Yugoslavia, Rising Ethnic Strife Brings Fears of Worse Civil Conflict," *NYT*, November 1 1987. On the background, see Vickers, op. cit.
67. Jeffrey Smith, "A Den of Thieves and Tax Cheats," *WP Weekly*, January 3 2000.
68. Peter Finn, "A new torture visits Kosovo: imported sex slaves," *WP*, April 30; Barbara Crossette, "U.N. Warns That Trafficking in Human Beings Is Growing," *NYT*, June 25 2000.
69. Elizabeth Sullivan, *Cleveland Plain Dealer*, April 3; BBC Summary of World Broadcasts, March 25 2000.
70. Lucian Kim, "Danube trade blocked by bridges," *CSM*, October 6; John Reed, "Since Kosovo War, the Danube Waltz Has Slowed to a Crawl," *WSJ*, September 20 1999. For an attempt to assess the regional costs, and others, see Ted Galen Carpenter, ed., *NATO's Empty Victory* (Washington: CATO Institute, 2000).
71. *Moscow Times*, July 9 1999.
72. Michael Littlejohns, "Annan criticises Nato's action in Kosovo," *Financial Times*, September 9 1999.

CHAPTER FOUR

Human Rights in the New Millennium

Before trying to address the current state of human rights, it is worth considering what is admitted into that sacred canon. The question constantly arises, quite concretely. For example, ten days ago, on the International Day for the Eradication of Poverty, when Amnesty International declared that "Poverty is the world's worst human rights crisis." Or two days before that, on World Food Day, when the UN food agency reported that the number of people going hungry rose to over 1 billion, while rich countries sharply cut back food aid because of the priority of bailing out banks, and Oxfam reported that 16,000 children are dying every day from hunger-related causes – that is twice Rwanda-level killing just among children, not for 100 days, but every day, and increasing. And the issues regularly arise even in the richest country in the world, where the question of whether health care is a human right is being hotly debated while some 45,000 people a year die from lack of insurance, and unknown numbers from utterly inadequate insurance, in the only industrial society I know of where health care is rationed by wealth, not need.

It is all too easy to add examples. In all these cases, the lives could be saved by a tiny fraction of the GDP of the rich countries, so the question is whether they recognize the right to life as among human rights.

There is a gold standard on human rights – the founding documents of the UN: the Charter and the Universal Declaration of Human Rights. The Charter guarantees the right to be protected from what was declared at Nuremberg to be the "supreme international crime," differing from other war crimes in that it encompasses all the evil that follows: the crime of aggression, which is reasonably well-defined. In practice, the Charter has long ago been revoked. Article 2(4) is in the wastebasket. There are sophisticated arguments in the international law literature to show that it doesn't mean what it says – when we carry out aggression, that is: no such questions arise when Russia or Saddam Hussein do.

The US has been, in large measure, the global sovereign since World War II, and remains so despite the increasing diversity of the global economy in past decades. Hence its practices are of great significance in considering the prospects for human rights. It is, for example, of great significance that the US is self-exempted from international law. To mention just one case of no slight import that took place in the real world, but not in official history, there is John F. Kennedy's armed attack against South Vietnam in 1962, an attack that initiated the most severe crimes of aggression since World War II.

Sometimes there have been candid explanations of the reasons for the US exemption from international law. One instructive case was during the US war against Nicaragua in the '80s – which, incidentally, falls quite precisely under "aggression" as defined at the Nuremberg Tribunal by Justice Robert Jackson, Chief of Counsel for the United States at Nuremberg, restated in an authoritative General Assembly resolution. As you know, Nicaragua brought a case against the US to the ICJ. The case was presented by Abram Chayes, a distinguished Harvard University law professor and former legal adviser to the State Department. Most of his case was rejected by the court on the grounds that in accepting ICJ jurisdiction in 1946, the US had entered a reservation excluding itself from prosecution under multilateral treaties, among them the UN and OAS Charters. The court therefore restricted its deliberations to customary international law and a bilateral US-Nicaragua treaty. Even on these very narrow grounds, the court charged Washington with "unlawful use of force" – in informal usage, international terrorism – and ordered it to terminate the crimes and pay substantial reparations, which would have gone far beyond paying off the huge debt that was strangling Nicaragua. The US dismissed the judgment, then vetoed two Security Council resolutions supporting it and calling on states to observe international law. It was helped by Britain, which abstained.

Congress at once passed bipartisan legislation to escalate the war. The court was dismissed as a "hostile forum" (*New York Times* editors), much as the US and Israel now dismiss the UN generally as biased and hostile because it does not always follow orders.

The court decision went further. It prohibited any form of intervention that interferes with the right of "choice of a political, economic, social and cultural system, and the formulation of policy." The judgment applies to many other crimes, among them the US assault against Cuba for fifty years, including extensive and acknowledged international terrorism and savage economic warfare.

US rejection of the court decision in the Nicaraguan case was explained by State Department legal adviser Abram Sofaer, now George Shultz Senior Fellow in Foreign Policy and National Security Affairs at the Hoover Institute, whose publications tell us that "Reagan's spirit seems to stride over the country, watching us like a warm and friendly ghost," the kind of words rarely heard outside of Pyongyang, and in this case Stanford University (though they are not alone in worship of the deity).

Sofaer explained that the majority of the world "often opposes the United States on important international questions," so that we must "reserve to ourselves the power to determine" which matters fall "essentially within the domestic jurisdiction of the United States, as determined by the United States" – in this case, international terrorism that practically destroyed the targeted country. Honest, and accurate. His explanation, and much else like it, merits more attention than it receives – that is, more than virtually zero.

There is not much point going on about the self-exemption of the powerful from international law because it is too obvious to those who are willing to look. Let us turn then to the second of the founding UN documents, the UD.

The rights I referred to earlier fall under socioeconomic rights, Article 25. But that article, too, is in the wastebasket. One leading academic specialist on these matters, Philip Alston, writes that after a brief detour caused by popular pressure in the 1970s, US human rights policy returned under Reagan to "the unqualified rejection of economic, social, and cultural 'rights' as rights" – that means unqualified rejection of two-thirds of the UD. It should be stressed that these provisions have exactly the same status as others. That has not been in question, at least in the international arena, since the UD was approved in 1948. It was emphasized again at the 2005 UN World Summit. Washington formally agreed, while rejecting the principle, under the usual veil of silence.

There have been some open expressions of utter contempt for the guarantees of socioeconomic rights. A case in point is Soviet UN Ambassador Andrei Vyshinsky, who dismissed them as just a "collection of pious phrases." He was joined by US Ambassador Jeane Kirkpatrick, recently honored by Condoleezza Rice as one of the stellar figures of American diplomacy. For Kirkpatrick, the socioeconomic provisions of the UD are "a letter to Santa Claus ... Neither nature, experience, nor probability informs these lists of 'entitlements,' which are subject to no constraints except those of the mind and appetite of their authors."

The same stand was elaborated by Paula Dobriansky, Undersecretary of State for Global Affairs under Bush II and Assistant Secretary of State for Human Rights and Human Affairs in the Reagan and Bush I administrations. In the latter capacity, she took pains to dispel what she called "myths" about human rights, the most salient being the myth that so-called "'economic and social rights' constitute human rights." She denounced the efforts to obfuscate human rights discourse by introducing these spurious rights – which are entrenched in the UD, formulated at US initiative, but explicitly rejected by Washington, not alone, of course.

Essentially the same view was expressed in 1990 by the US representative to the UN Commission on Human Rights, Ambassador Morris Abram, explaining Washington's solitary veto of the UN resolution on the Right to Development, which virtually repeated the socioeconomic provisions of the UD. These are not rights, Abram instructed the commission. They yield conclusions that "seem preposterous." Such ideas are "little more than an empty vessel into which vague hopes and inchoate expectations can be poured," and even a "dangerous incitement." The fundamental error of the proposed "right to development" is that it takes Article 25 of the UD to mean what it clearly states, not as a mere "letter to Santa Claus."

US practice conforms to these principles. The US scarcely ever even ratifies enabling conventions that put some teeth into the letter from Santa Claus. One example is the Convention on the Rights of the Child. It has been ratified by all countries other than the US and Somalia – which has no functioning government. Or the International Covenant on Civil and Political Rights, "the leading treaty for the protection" of the subcategory of rights that the West claims to uphold, to quote Human Rights Watch and the American Civil Liberties Union, in a joint report on US noncompliance with its provisions. Incidentally, that was in the halcyon days before George W. Bush poisoned the pure well. The Covenant was ratified, after a long delay, but only with provisions to render it inapplicable to the US. Ratification was "an empty act for Americans," the report concludes.

That is a considerable understatement. The few conventions that Washington ratifies are accompanied by reservations rendering them inapplicable to the US. That includes, among others, the Genocide Convention. A few years ago, the US appealed to that reservation in exempting itself from Yugo-slavia's case against NATO. The court agreed, correctly: The US reserves the right to commit genocide, as was reported, but with no comment.

Another example is the UN Convention Against Torture, the topic of considerable recent discussion. The rulings of Bush's Justice Department were bitterly condemned, with la-ments that under Bush "we have lost our way." But few asked what way we had lost. Torture has been routine practice from the early days of the conquest of the national territory, and then beyond, as imperial ventures extended to the Philippines, Haiti, and elsewhere. And, of course, torture was among the least of the many crimes that have darkened US history, much as in the case of other great powers. Accordingly, it was surpris-ing to see the reactions even by some of the most eloquent and forthright critics of Bush malfeasance: for example, that we used to be "a nation of moral ideals" and never before Bush "have our leaders so utterly betrayed everything our nation stands for" (Paul Krugman). To say the least, that common view reflects a rather slanted version of history.

Furthermore, it is far from clear that the Bush Justice Department violated US law. That was pointed out by legal scholar Sanford Levinson, who observed that there is a legal basis for rulings authorizing torture. Washington did ratify the anti-torture convention, but only after the Senate provided what Levinson calls a more "interrogator-friendly" definition of torture than in the convention, a version used by the President's legal advisers in justifying the practices in Guantánamo, Iraq, Afghanistan, and who knows where else; not to speak of unknown numbers sent by "rendition" to countries where torture is virtually guaranteed – practices extended under Obama, along with other severe Bush administration violations of elementary human rights, like denial of habeas corpus. In this case, the matter is still in the courts, where Obama is appealing a decision by a hard-line Bush appointee, who held that the Supreme Court ruling on Guantánamo applies also to the US prison at Bagram airbase in Afghanistan. Obama's Justice Department maintains that the US government must be authorized to kidnap people anywhere in the world and send them into its secret prison systems without charges or rights, perhaps an indication of the prospects for human rights in the new millennium.

Fuller significant facts about torture are discussed by historian Alfred McCoy, the author of some of the most important works on the history of torture. McCoy points out that the highly sophisticated CIA torture paradigm developed in the 1950s keeps primarily to mental torture, not crude physical torture, which is considered less effective in turning people into pliant vegetables. The CIA was basing itself on the "KGB's most devastating torture technique" and recent experimental work, McCoy writes. He reviews how the Reagan administration revised the UN Torture Convention "with four detailed diplomatic 'reservations' focused on just one word in the convention's 26 printed pages," the word "mental." These reservations redefined torture to exclude the techniques refined by the CIA and applied worldwide. When Clinton sent the UN Convention to Congress for ratification in 1994, he included the Reagan reservations. The President and Congress therefore exempted the core of the CIA torture paradigm from the US interpretation of the Torture Convention; and those reservations, McCoy observes, were "reproduced verbatim in domestic legislation enacted to give legal force to the UN Convention." That, he says, is the "political land mine" that "detonated with such phenomenal force" in the Abu Ghraib scandal and in the shameful Military Commissions act that was passed with bipartisan support in 2006 – and has been renewed by Obama, in slightly different form.

So protection from torture goes the way of socioeconomic and cultural rights: It does not enter into the human rights canon.

There are other revealing examples. To select one instructive case, for 60 years the US has failed to ratify the core principle of international labor law, which guarantees freedom of association. Legal analysts call it "the untouchable treaty in American politics," and observe that there has never even been any debate about the matter. This is particularly striking alongside the intense dedication to enforcement of rights of corporations, as in safeguarding monopoly pricing rights of unprecedented scale, a core element of the highly protectionist World Trade Organization system.

Such contrasts lead to situations that are highly revealing about the prospects for human rights. Right now, the two American political parties are competing to see which can uphold more fervently its dedication to the sadistic doctrine that undocumented immigrants must be denied health care. Their stand is consistent with the legal principle, established by the Supreme Court, that these creatures are not "persons" under the law, hence are not entitled to the rights granted to persons. And at the very same moment, the court is considering the question of whether corporations should be permitted to purchase elections openly instead of doing so only in more indirect ways – a complex constitutional matter because the courts have determined that unlike undocumented immigrants, corporations are real persons under the law, and in fact have rights far beyond those of persons of flesh and blood, including rights granted by the mislabelled "free trade agreements." These revealing coincidences elicit no comment. The law is indeed a solemn and majestic affair.

I do not want to suggest that nothing has improved with regard to concern for human rights. A significant HR culture has developed among the general population, and that has had consequences that governments and other power systems have been unable to ignore completely, a very important matter.

Let's turn to the interesting question of how official doctrines have evolved since the collapse of the USSR. Prior to that, there was a reflexive justification for any act of violence: forceful intervention, subversion, sabotage, terror, and other prima facie violations of international law and human rights. The Russians are coming, period. But with the fall of the Berlin

Wall, now being commemorated, that option was gone. The Bush I administration responded immediately with a National Security Strategy and a military ("defense") budget, which announced that nothing was about to change. Therefore, a new pretext would be needed — and as if by magic, one was provided by the intellectual community. The 1990s were declared to be the opening of a new era in the West, dedicated to the "emerging norm of humanitarian intervention." The new era was accompanied by an impressive chorus of self-glorification, which may have no counterpart in intellectual history. It peaked as the US-UK prepared to bomb Serbia, an attack featured in Western discourse as the jewel in the crown of the "emerging norm," when the US was at the "height of its glory," in a "noble phase" of its foreign policy with a "saintly glow," acting from "altruism alone" in leading the "enlightened states" on their missions of mercy, led by the "idealistic New World bent on ending inhumanity," opening a new page of history by acting on "principles and values" alone for the first time — to cite just a few of the accolades by eminent Western intellectuals.

There were a few difficulties confronting the flattering self-image that was constructed with such enthusiasm. One problem was that the traditional victims of Western intervention vigorously objected. The meeting of the South Summit of 133 states, convened in April 2000, issued a declaration, surely with the bombing of Serbia in mind, rejecting "the so-called 'right' of humanitarian intervention, which has no legal basis in the United Nations Charter or in the general principles of international law." The wording reaffirms the UN Declaration on

Friendly Relations of 1970. The wording was repeated in later years, among other occasions at the Ministerial Meeting of the Non-aligned Movement in Malaysia in 2006, again representing the traditional victims in Asia, Africa, Latin America, and the Arab world. The same conclusion was drawn in 2004 by the high-level UN Panel on Threats, Challenges and Change, with prominent Western figures participating. The panel adopted the view of the ICJ and the Non-aligned Movement, concluding that "Article 51 [of the Charter] needs neither extension nor restriction of its long-understood scope." The panel added that "For those impatient with such a response," which, of course, bars the jewel in the crown and many other current acts of Western violence, "the answer must be that, in a world full of perceived potential threats, the risk to the global order and the norm of nonintervention on which it continues to be based is simply too great for the legality of unilateral preventive action, as distinct from collectively endorsed action, to be accepted. Allowing one to so act is to allow all" – which is, of course, unthinkable. The same position was adopted by the UN World Summit a year later, again affirming the unchanging position of the Global South, the traditional victims.

Evidently, "humanitarian intervention" wouldn't quite do, though it lingers. Something else was needed, and lo and behold, a new doctrine emerged, just in time: "Responsibility to Protect," familiarly known as R2P, now the topic of a substantial literature, many conferences, new organizations and journals, and much praise. The praise is justified, at least in one respect. We may recall Gandhi's response to the question of what he thought about Western civilization. He's alleged to have said "It would be a good idea." And the same holds of R2P. It would be a good idea.

On that much, everyone should agree. But then the usual problems arise. Just what is R2P, and when does it apply?

On the first question – what is R2P? – there are two versions, commonly conflated, though they differ radically. One is the position of the Global South, formulated in the 2005 UN World Summit. A very different position is articulated in the founding document of R2P, the Report of the International Commission on Intervention and State Sovereignty on Responsibility to Protect, of which the leading figure and spokesperson is Australia's Gareth Evans.

It is important to distinguish these two radically different conceptions. The World Summit basically reiterated positions already adopted by the UN, at most focusing more sharply on certain components of them. The summit reiterates the stand of the South and the High Level Panel that forceful action can only be carried out under Security Council authorization, though it allowed an exception for states of the African Union, granted a qualified right of intervention within the AU itself. If that exception were generalized, the consequences would be interesting. For example, Latin American countries would be authorized to carry out large-scale terror in the US to protect victims of US violence in the hemisphere. We can therefore put the AU exception aside, though it is commonly adduced by proponents of R2P to show that it is not an instrument of imperialism, but rather is rooted in the South – as it is, in the World Summit version of R2P.

The crucial paragraphs of the summit declaration, all agree, are 138 and 139. Their provisions had not been seriously con-

tested, and in fact had been affirmed and implemented, specifically with regard to apartheid South Africa. Furthermore, the
Security Council had already determined that it can even use
force under Chapter VII to end massive human rights abuses,
civil war, and violation of civil liberties: Resolutions 925, 929,
940, mid-1994. And, as analysts have rightly observed, "most
states are signatories to conventions that legally oblige them
to respect the human rights of their citizens," as resolved again
by the summit declaration. It is therefore not at all surprising
that the General Assembly adopted the summit declaration,
while the sharp North-South split on "the so-called 'right' of
humanitarian intervention" persisted without change.

The second version of R2P, in the Evans Report, differs
fundamentally from the summit declaration. In its crucial
paragraph, the commission considers the situation in which
"the Security Council rejects a proposal or fails to deal with
it in a reasonable time." In that case, the report authorizes
"action within area of jurisdiction by regional or sub-regional
organizations under Chapter VIII of the Charter, subject
to their seeking subsequent authorization from the Security
Council." This paragraph is plainly intended to apply retrospectively to the bombing of Serbia, just what was forcefully
rejected by the global South and the World Summit version
of R2P. This provision of the Evans Commission effectively
authorizes the powerful to use force at will. The reason is
clear: the powerful unilaterally determine their own "area
of jurisdiction." The OAS and AU cannot do so, but NATO
can, and does. NATO unilaterally determined that its "area
of jurisdiction" includes the Balkans – but, interestingly, not

NATO itself, where shocking crimes were committed against Kurds in southeastern Turkey through the 1990s, all off the agenda because of the decisive military support for them by the leader of the free world, peaking in the very year when it was praised for the "noble phase" of its foreign policy with "a saintly glow"; and, of course, with the aid of other NATO powers. NATO later determined that its "area of jurisdiction" extends to Afghanistan. And well beyond. Secretary-General Jaap de Hoop Scheffer informed a NATO meeting in 2007 that "NATO troops have to guard pipelines that transport oil and gas that is directed for the West," and more generally have to protect sea routes used by tankers and other "crucial infrastructure" of the energy system. The expansive rights accorded by the Evans Commission are in practice restricted to NATO alone, radically violating the principles adopted by the World Summit. They explicitly open the door wide for resort to R2P as a weapon of imperial intervention at will.

Let's turn to the second question: How is R2P applied in practice? The answer will surprise no one who has the slightest familiarity with history or elementary understanding of the structure of power. I will not run through the highly selective application, but consider just a few examples. There is no thought of devoting pennies to protect the huge numbers dying from hunger and lack of health care, or deprivation of other "rights" that are dismissed as "myths" and "dangerous incitement" by Washington. Protected populations are also barred from protection, among them the victims of US-Israeli attack in Gaza, who are protected persons under the Geneva conventions. Those who are the direct responsibility of the Security

Council also are unable to appeal to R2P; for example, Iraqis subjected to murderous sanctions under the saintly glow of Clinton's policies, and Blair's, sanctions that were condemned as genocidal by the administrators of the UN programs, the respected international diplomats Denis Halliday and Hans von Sponeck, both of whom resigned in protest for that reason. Or the victims of the worst massacres of recent years, in the Eastern Congo, where only the ultra-cynical might suspect that the neglect has something to do with the fact that the worst offender is US ally Rwanda, and that multinationals are making a mint from robbing the region's rich mineral resources with the crucial aid of the militias tearing the place to shreds. And on, and on, just as the rational would expect.

There is also a lot to say about the jewel in the crown, Kosovo, but in England that (and the Balkans generally) is a matter of fanatic religious doctrine, much more extreme than that evoked by Israel in the US, so one cannot talk about it without a lot of time and a full apparatus of footnotes, and even that only evokes impressive tantrums, an interesting story that I'll put aside.

R2P is rather like "democracy promotion." The leading scholar/advocate of this cause, neo-Reaganite Thomas Carothers, ruefully concludes from his careful inquiries that the US promotes democracy if and only if that stance conforms to strategic and economic interests, a pattern that runs through all administrations. Leaders are "schizophrenic," he concludes with puzzlement. Critics sometimes speak of "double standards."

But there is no puzzle, and there is a single standard. The standard was described accurately enough by Adam Smith, speaking of England in his day, where the "merchants and manufacturers" were the "principal architects" of policy and made sure that their own interests had "been most peculiarly attended to," however "grievous" the effect on others, including the people of England, but much more so the victims of "the savage injustice of the Europeans," particularly the victims of England in India, his prime concern. Much has changed since his day, but the principle remains.

There was great indignation last summer when General Assembly President Miguel D'Escoto called a session devoted to R2P. *The Economist* warned of the danger that "An angry, inconclusive General Assembly debate" might undermine this "idealistic effort to establish a new humanitarian principle," now "coming under attack at the United Nations" – an attack that the journal conjured up: as I mentioned, virtually no one opposes R2P in the form adopted at the World Summit, though there is very good reason to oppose the Evans Commission version and the selective application of the summit declaration. *The Economist* editors were encouraged, however, that the angry opponents they invented (of whom I was one, incidentally) would at least be countered by one panel member, "Gareth Evans, a former Australian foreign minister and roving global troubleshooter, [who] makes a bold but passionate claim on behalf of a three-word expression which (in quite large part thanks to his efforts) now belongs to the language of diplomacy: the 'responsibility to protect.'" Their ode to Evans is accompanied by a picture showing him with his hand on his face, grieving that his bold and passionate claim is coming under threat: the subtitle reads: "a lifelong passion to protect."

The journal chose not to run a different picture, from about the same time, which sheds some light on this lifelong passion. It shows Evans with his Indonesian counterpart Ali Alatas, joyously celebrating the treaty they had just signed granting Australia the right to rob the oil resources of what the treaty calls "the Indonesian Province of East Timor." The treaty offered nothing to the remnants who survived the Western-backed onslaught on East Timor. It is furthermore "the only legal agreement anywhere in the world that effectively recognizes Indonesia's right to rule East Timor," the Australian press reported.

The Evans-Alatas picture is familiar among those who happen to see a problem when their own countries provide the decisive support for aggression that led to one of the worst slaughters of the modern period, continuing right through the chorus of self-congratulation in 1999 at a level beyond Kosovo before the NATO bombing, and, of course, the past record far exceeded the atrocities of the Balkans. It is an uncomfortable topic, so the factual record is best avoided, or denied, as is regularly done, sometimes in remarkable ways that I will not review.

The journal's choice of a photograph should come as no surprise. Twenty years earlier, when the basic facts of the near-genocidal slaughter carried out with US-UK support were well-known, the editors described the great mass murderer and torturer Suharto as "at heart benign" – toward foreign investors, at least – while denouncing the "propagandists for the guerrillas" in East Timor and Irian Jaya with their "talk of the army's savagery and use of torture," including the Church in East Timor, thousands of refugees in Australia and Portugal, Western diplomats and journalists who had chosen to see, the most respected international human rights monitors, and more recently a UN-backed truth commission, all "propagandists" rather than intrepid champions of human rights – because they had quite the wrong story to tell. And who could be a more noble and passionate supporter of R2P than the person who celebrated his achievement of granting Australia the rights to the sole resources of the territory brutalized with Australian support, while explaining that it matters little because "the world is a pretty unfair place, littered with examples of acquisition by force." True enough, a matter that appears to be of slight concern to the advocates of selective R2P, and also to the Western intellectuals who feign great indignation at the other fellow's crimes, while easily condoning or denying their own, updating a leading theme of the inglorious history of intellectuals from the earliest records.

What then are the hopes for human rights in the new millennium? I think the answer is the one that reverberates through history, including recent years. It is not a law of nature that we have to subordinate ourselves to the violence and deceit of the "principal architects" of policy and the doctrinal manipulation of the servants of power. As in the past, an aroused and organized public can carve out space for authentic concern for human rights – including R2P – today, more easily than ever because we can benefit from the legacy of past struggles and their achievements.

Acknowledgments

Chapter 2 is expanded from "'Feu vert' occidental pour les massacres," *Le Monde diplomatique,* October 1999, and "The United States, East Timor, and Intervention" in the *Bulletin of Concerned Asian Scholars*; it also appears in a different form in Richard Tanter, Mark Selden, and Stephen Shalom, eds., *East Timor, Indonesia, and the World Community* (Boulder CO: Rowman & Littlefield, 2000).

Chapter 3 is expanded from the Afterword to the French edition of my *The New Military Humanism* (Lausanne: Page Deux, 2000), which also appears in other translations and in *Z Magazine,* April/May 2000.

Chapter 4 is the transcript of a lecture given at the London School of Economics and Political Science on October 29, 2009.

INDEX